12/22

Still Stace

My Gay Christian Coming-of-Age Story

Stacey Chomiak

beaming books

MINNEAPOLIS

Published in 2021 by Beaming Books, an imprint of 1517 Media. All rights reserved. No part of this book may be reproduced without the written permission of the publisher. Email copyright@1517.media. Printed in the United States of America.

27 26 25 24 23 22 21   2 3 4 5 6 7 8 9

Hardcover ISBN: 978-1-5064-6951-5
EBook ISBN: 978-1-5064-6952-2

Library of Congress Cataloging-in-Publication Data

Names: Chomiak, Stacey, author.
Title: Still Stace : my gay Christian coming of age story / by Stacey
  Chomiak.
Description: Minneapolis, MN : Beaming Books, 2021. | Audience: Ages 13-18
  | Summary: "An artist's captivating and quirky illustrated coming-of-age
  memoir of surprising first love, coming out, and coming to embrace her
  queer Christian identity"-- Provided by publisher.
Identifiers: LCCN 2020045210 (print) | LCCN 2020045211 (ebook) | ISBN
  9781506469515 (hardcover) | ISBN 9781506469522 (ebook)
Subjects: LCSH: Chomiak, Stacey--Juvenile literature. | Christian
  biography--Manitoba--Winnipeg--Juvenile literature. |
  Lesbians--Manitoba--Winnipeg--Biography--Juvenile literature. |
  Homosexuality--Religious aspects--Christianity--Juvenile literature.
Classification: LCC BR1725.C465 A3 2021 (print) | LCC BR1725.C465 (ebook)
  | DDC 270.092 [B]--dc23
LC record available at https://lccn.loc.gov/2020045210
LC ebook record available at https://lccn.loc.gov/2020045211

VN0004589; 9781506469515; AUG2021

Beaming Books
PO Box 1209
Minneapolis, MN 55440-1209
Beamingbooks.com

For Tams.

You held the thread of my humanity

until I could find it again.

Author's Note

This is my story of growing up and wrestling with my faith and sexuality. I tried to be as honest and vulnerable as possible, to convey the intense struggle and deep shame LGBTQ people of faith carry both within themselves and with their families.

Though it was tough to share, I decided to write about my early sexual experiences, because I don't think sex is talked about enough in LGBTQ Christian spaces. Shame in faith communities is incredibly powerful, and I would be happy to take away a little bit of that stigma.

Everything that happens in this story is to the best of my memory. The names of my friends and people I dated have been changed to protect their privacy. All of the dialogue has been reconstructed from my memory and my diaries, but is not word for word. I have also included excerpts from my prayer journals, since often the rawest parts of my struggle were only visible on those pages.

I hope that you will see yourself and your journey reflected in these pages so that, maybe, you will feel less alone.

Dear younger (gay) Stace,

I wish you had known that you were already whole.

You didn't need fixing.

Can we go back to those times I could hear your heart breaking?

Can we try to heal together?

Can I show you how, after the years of struggling with your faith and sexuality and believing you had to choose, you found something you didn't know was possible: peace.

But first, let's go back to the beginning. . .

Chapter 1

I gazed across the water from my spot on the edge of the dock. I ran my fingers over the rough wood, still warm from soaking in the day's sunshine. As I breathed deeply, the fragrant smell of pine trees coming across the lake made me smile. How I loved this place.

Every summer since I was eight, I'd spent a week at Calvary Temple Youth Camp in Whiteshell Provincial Park, Manitoba. It was my favorite place on earth. Spending a week with the other girls from youth group having fun and learning about Jesus was something I looked forward to all year. Every summer when I set foot onto the grounds, the familiar smell of the lake coming in on the breeze brought back every memory I'd ever had of camp. The silly songs and endless laughter. The late-night conversations about life and faith. Swimming in the lake. Doing arts and crafts. Playing Bible trivia. I loved learning from the counselors and discovering new things about Jesus.

My Christian faith was the main focus of the week. Christianity made sense, and it gave me purpose and life. I didn't just pretend to like Christianity—I was all in. I had grown up in this faith, and even now that I was in my teens, it was one of the things in my life that fit. Or actually, everything in my life fit around it.

I was painfully earnest about my faith, always wearing a small silver cross around my neck and excited to talk about the newest Christian music album. I loved the authenticity that rang true deep inside, and I loved the sense of community I always had with my camp and church friends. And here at camp, where one week felt like three months, my faith was challenged, supported, and encouraged.

One summer stands out above the rest. I was sixteen and couldn't stop thinking about my friend Joanna. I sat there in the dining hall eating my favorite camp side dish of scalloped potatoes, daydreaming about her long,

chestnut hair and hazel eyes. I had met her the year before in youth group. And now we were here together at camp. After lunch we were going to go swimming, and for some reason I felt really nervous. We had been spending a lot of time together already that week, so I wasn't sure why the thought of going swimming with her was making my stomach do flip-flops.

The day before, we had been in her cabin doing devotions, talking about why *The Message* version of the Bible was better than other translations. That morning, we had volunteered to partner together for the next chapel skit. We had picked the new Crystal Lewis song, "People Get Ready, Jesus Is Comin'," and it was going to be amazing.

I finished my lunch and quickly changed into my swimsuit. I was pretty self-conscious lately about being chubby; I wished I was thinner. But my friends were all different sizes, so I tried not to worry about it too much. I made my way down the huge rock face toward the lake front. I could see Joanna from a distance, sitting on the dock, happily chatting with a girl from her cabin. She noticed me coming, and her face broke out in a big smile. When she waved me over, my heart started to race. I felt my cheeks turning red. *What is happening?*

"Hi, Stace! Man, it's so hot right now. Wanna just jump in?"

I grinned. "Yes, let's do it!"

We threw our towels onto the dock and raced to the edge. I jumped into the refreshing lake water and let my body be suspended under the surface for a few seconds. Being submerged in water made it feel like time was standing still.

Soon a larger group of girls joined us, and we took turns clambering up on the dock and jumping back into the water, laughing at our huge splashes. As I treaded water across from Joanna, I noticed the light bouncing off the surface of the water onto her face, and my stomach felt . . . something.

Why can't she and I just hang out the rest of the week?

After Joanna left, I stayed back at the beach, all wrapped up in my oversized watermelon towel. I stared out at the water, the waves making a melodic lapping sound against the dock. I started daydreaming. About her. Again. I dug my toes into the warm sand. I had never felt drawn to someone in this way before. It wasn't a crush like I knew I was supposed to have for boys. Those sorts of feelings were reserved for my future husband.

I had it all planned out. Since I loved Christian music and church, I was obviously going to marry a floppy-haired music-slash-youth pastor with a casual sense of style and a great sense of humor. I hadn't met any boys I liked yet. I hadn't felt any attraction to boys at all so far, which meant I must be pretty strong in the resisting-temptation department. I mean, I *was* a perfectionist in most areas of my life, so maybe I was already passing Temptation 101 with flying colors?

I *did* know all the words to the songs we sang in chapel—and most of the Bible verses we were supposed to memorize—so maybe my mind was just so full of Jesus, it had no room for temptation? *(Is that why they make us memorize those verses?)*

Or maybe I just hadn't met the right guy yet. When I was thirteen, a boy in my class asked me out to a school dance. It totally threw me off and I freaked out. I told him that my parents didn't allow me to go to dances. Which sounded true, because they were really, really conservative. But the truth was I just didn't feel comfortable going to a dance. I wasn't ready. Now that I was sixteen, maybe I'd find someone I wanted to go out with.

But at this all-girls' week of summer camp, flirting with boys wasn't really an option. Which was fine by me—I could just enjoy spending time with Joanna.

I stood up, rubbing my towel over my wet hair. A shower was all I needed to rinse these confusing thoughts from my mind. Camp always brought up so many emotions. I was just getting them all mixed up.

Chapter 2

Back home in Winnipeg after camp, Joanna and I continued to hang out. She lived nearby in another suburb. Since she had her driver's license, she could pop over in her little hatchback. Lately she had been picking me up for youth group. It was pretty cool to have a friend who could drive.

One day we were at my house, sitting on the floor of my bedroom. Avalon's "Picture Perfect World" was playing on my stereo, with a bunch more Christian music CD's strewn about haphazardly. Joanna and I had so much in common, and we were quickly becoming best friends.

"Who's cooler—dc Talk or Newsboys?" Joanna held the CD's up in front of my face, waving them back and forth. "Come onnnn, you gotta choose just one!" She giggled.

"Oh man, I don't know!" I smiled enthusiastically back at her. "Okay, maybe dc Talk because of their *Jesus Freak* album?"

"Yeah, I agree. Okay, let's read that article in *Brio*!"

9

Brio was a pop-culture magazine for Christian teens. I loved the down-to-earth articles about beauty and self-care combined with interviews with Christian music artists and funny stories. Joanna got up to grab the magazine across the room. When she returned, she sat so close to me that her thigh was against my thigh. Her arm dropped, and her upper body leaned into me as she opened the magazine. I didn't move away. I liked being this close to her. Maybe it was just a best friend thing.

"Hey Jo, guess what?" I was on my bed fidgeting with the red cord of my Mickey Mouse phone. "My mom said we could have a sleepover in the motorhome tonight!"

"Awesome! I'll pack up and be right over!"

I hung up and stared at the smooth white ceiling with a smile. This was going to be so fun. We could talk all night.

Sharing a bed in the motorhome later that evening, neither of us noticed that it was getting really late. We had this space all to ourselves, and it was so nice that my younger brother, Cody, or my parents wouldn't barge in. I didn't want to go to sleep yet. Sleep was so boring.

We lay side by side, chatting less as it got later, enjoying the comfortable lulls to listen to music. Jaci Velasquez's latest album played softly in the background. I realized as I lay there that I suddenly felt closer to Joanna than to anyone else. She turned to face me.

"You know, Stace, I really care about you." Her voice was soft. I smiled.

"I really care about you too, Jo." My body tingled. Something was about to happen, and I didn't want to do anything to disrupt it.

Joanna leaned over and kissed my forehead. A rush of emotions flowed from where her lips had touched my skin. I didn't understand what was happening, but I liked it. I kept very still.

I felt her face travel down, and she kissed the tip of my nose. *Keep going.* Her face traveled a little further down and our lips met. I closed my eyes as we began to kiss. At the sensation of her lips against mine, my heart spun wildly inside my chest and I lost my breath. I had never, *ever* felt this before.

My head emptied of all ability to think. I was completely lost and floating in the moment, our lips pressed together, her hand gently touching my face and pulling me in. Time, space, words . . . meant nothing.

We stopped kissing a few minutes later. I took a deep breath to steady myself. I didn't know where to look. I felt her hot breath on my cheek. My head felt fuzzy, and I couldn't seem to form words.

Joanna whispered first. "I'm sorry if that—"

"No, it's okay." I wanted to reassure her, even though my feelings of euphoria were beginning to mingle with thick guilt. Kissing Joanna was definitely *not* the Christian thing to do. But I couldn't stop myself, or this intense feeling in my body.

Before I could think any more, I reached up and pulled her face in again, her lips back onto mine. Losing my breath. I was overtaken with the spinning in my chest. *What is this feeling?* Her lips felt so soft against mine. It felt so natural, even though I had never kissed anyone before. I knew the guilt was trying to warn me this was going to become a major problem. *Why does it feel so good to kiss a girl?*

We didn't do much sleeping or talking for the next few hours. My body never felt more awake. I only knew it was close to morning when I heard the birds chirping outside the window.

Chapter 3

Winnipeg, Manitoba

My basketball ricocheted off the backboard in our driveway, and I jumped to the side to catch it. I was playing by myself a lot lately so I could think. My mind was clearer when my body was moving. I needed to understand more about these feelings, this confusion inside.

Joanna and I kept hanging out since our first kiss a few months ago, and whenever we were alone, it was impossible not to kiss. I had no words for this. Except maybe sin? What would our friends at youth group say if they found out? What would my parents say? What would *Jesus* say? I could barely think about it.

When we weren't together, I thought about kissing her. What it felt like. What it did to my body. But then my heart, mind, and soul felt like they'd been drenched by an enormous pitcher of shame. How could I let this happen? Worse yet—How can I enjoy it so much? Christian girls should not kiss other Christian girls—not the way they are supposed to kiss their boyfriends.

Wait—is *this* temptation?

The storefront lights blurred together as we drove through downtown Winnipeg. It was late, and there wasn't much traffic.

"What did Lisa mean by that, do you think?" I asked Joanna as she drove.

"Nothing, I'm sure. She said she noticed we've been hanging out a lot together lately. It's no big deal." She put her hand on my knee. *I shouldn't love it when she touches me but I do.*

"Okay, I'm just paranoid. I don't want anyone finding out about . . . this. Do you?" I said.

"Don't worry, Stace. It's fine. No one suspects anything." She grabbed my hand and squeezed it. I didn't let go.

We pulled into Joanna's grandmother's driveway across town. Joanna was living with her grandma because she didn't have a great relationship with her mom. My parents knew I was planning to sleep over there after youth group.

I went into her bathroom to change into my pajamas because I was too shy to change in front of anyone. I was really tired. We had stayed too late talking with our friends at church. But when I was in Joanna's big bed and I could feel her next to me, my body started to wake up. Maybe I could ignore it.

I turned over, my back to her. "Night, Jo. Have a good sleep."

She gently tugged on my shoulder, turning me toward her.

"Hey, come here . . ." Before I knew it her lips were on mine, and I was powerless. I couldn't resist this. I felt the guilt rise up, but this other feeling in my body was much stronger.

So far, we had only been kissing. Even *French* kissing, which I thought would be gross. Actually, it was quite wonderful. But French kissing was not enough for what my body was wanting right now. I wanted more.

I leaned in and wrapped my arms around her. I pulled her body close as we kissed, feeling her chest against mine through our pajama tops. My whole body was electric and tingling. I don't know why, but it felt right to slowly roll her over and lie on top of her. I felt her warm body under mine and suddenly panicked that I was too heavy.

"Is this okay?" I whispered into her ear, my heart pounding out of my chest.

"Yes. Keep going . . ." She pulled my lips back onto hers.

This passion I felt was blinding.

I went into her pajama top with my hands and felt her soft warm skin. She did the same to me. Her touch left goose bumps on my skin.

For a split second I wondered why I wasn't embarrassed, but I couldn't hold on to that thought for long. We kept kissing, and something in my body was building, something I had no control over. The feeling was all consuming—it cut off my ability to think about anything else. Soon I could no longer hold it back, and suddenly I felt an explosion of pleasure.

What is this?!

As I caught my breath and my body started to calm, I felt hers tense and she pulled me tighter. I had no idea what had just happened, but it seemed to have happened to both of us.

As my pulse began to slow, other thoughts came back into focus. So did the *immense* guilt. *What are we doing? What am I doing?* I rolled over to lie beside her.

I was overwhelmed by an entirely new level of shame.

Sitting on my bed, my legs gathered up in front of me for safety, I felt so lost. I took out my journal and pen from my bedside table. A thick fog of embarrassment and guilt surrounded me.

Now that Joanna and I had done more than kissing, this shame I felt was inescapable and paralyzing. I normally felt better when I could release things onto paper. But lately, my journaling only led to more questions and bigger fears.

Jesus, you know I honestly want to live a life pleasing to you, right? I really do. But sometimes temptation and being confused get in the way. Father, some things have happened lately that I'm not sure about. Joanna and I have talked about it; we want to do what's right in your eyes. It's just so hard. Please forgive me if I am in sin now. Jesus, cleanse me and open my eyes to what you want.

I stopped writing and chewed on the end of my pen. I really hoped Jesus read my prayer journal often.

I was so distracted by what Joanna and I had shared a few nights ago. It was the most intense thing I had ever felt. What was that? It couldn't be sex. Sex was only possible between a man and a woman, so I was safe. I didn't know much, but I knew my friends were all very curious about what sex would be like when they got married. If it felt anything like that . . . then, yeah. I was very curious now too.

I had been arguing with myself these last few months, but this proved it. I was definitely struggling with *something*. Struggling with . . . being attracted to girls. I needed to do some research, and everyone at church says all of life's answers are in the Bible.

I searched my room for all of the Bibles I owned and piled them on my bed. My little pale pink Bible, with its precious crinkly pages that I had received at my baby dedication. I sometimes pulled it out to gingerly feel the pages between my fingers. My colorful NIV Study Bible with notes jotted in the margins. My leather-bound King James Bible with carefully underlined verses. My hopeful and trendy *The Message*.

Desperately, I searched them all. Maybe a different translation would set me free from this mess. Perhaps one of them would have clues or answers, or would say something hopeful about what I felt. Or how I got here.

I flipped to the back of my NIV Study Bible and combed through the glossary of terms. My eyes jumped to a word I had only seen once before, in a letter my mom wrote to my teacher, excusing me from sex-ed class.

Homosexuality.

Fear rumbled through my body. Tucked away in a very dark and extremely small space in my brain, I remembered that I had only heard that word spoken in shocked whispers. I could barely say it silently inside my head, for fear Cody or my parents might hear. I needed to learn more. *This is so terrifyingly lonely.*

Chapter 4

A couple months passed, and a big group of us were at a restaurant late one Friday night after youth group, celebrating my seventeenth birthday. We were a rousing crew, enjoying our iced teas and plates of spicy fries. My friends made me laugh and made me feel loved. But I was so confused inside. Studying the Bible in secret had been no help. Joanna sat beside me, laughing at a joke with our friend Lisa. She acted like my other friends when we were all together. But we both knew she wasn't just a friend. I desperately needed to understand this.

The only place I knew to get more information was the library.

The next morning, off I went, wearing my most boring, beige outfit so as not to draw any attention. If anyone asked, I would say I was researching a project for school—but the only project on my mind was "Project Why Am I Liking Girls?"

I did a quick walk around the library, trying to look casual and breezy. I needed to make sure no one I knew was there. I couldn't risk someone finding out my biggest, most horrifying secret.

I was almost too scared to look it up. But as I heaved a massive dictionary onto the desk in a corner of the sun-filled library, my fingers furiously thumbed to "H." My eyes found it quickly, as if a magnet had pulled them there.

Homosexuality. I read the word silently, and then immediately looked up, expecting a huge alarm bell to sound and everyone to come running, mouths open in anger and disgust. I took a deep breath, realizing no one was even close by, and returned to the word in question.

Homosexuality: the quality or characteristic of being sexually attracted solely to people of one's own sex.

Oh no. When I read that, something resonated inside—something I identified with. I closed my eyes, partly wishing I hadn't read those words, but also grateful for some proper understanding. I read the entry again, slower this time.

Homosexuality: the quality or characteristic of being sexually attracted solely to people of one's own sex. See: lesbianism..

What? What is lesbianism?

Now the curious part of me needed to know. It rose up and shoved aside the fear part. I flipped over to "L" as fast as humanly possible. *Lesbianism: sexual attraction or sexual activity between women.*

My mind flashed to lying on top of Joanna while we kissed, and the vibration of fear and embarrassment was almost too much. It made me want to throw the dictionary across the room. Intense shame sloshed around in my body. Is *that* what that was? *Sexual activity between women? Lesbianism?!*

No, it couldn't be. I touched the silver cross around my neck and pulled it back and forth on the chain, trying to calm myself.

Kissing—and doing more—

with Joanna was wrong, I knew that. Maybe I was just giving in to some weak moments, but lesbianism? Not me, no way, that's not me. I'm Stace. Good kid, good person, good Christian. I didn't know much about those words, but I knew they only meant sin. Big, huge, devastating sin. I could feel what people in church would think and say, and it made me want to crawl in a hole.

I have to do everything I can to stay far, far away.

A few days later in the privacy of Joanna's bedroom, we tried talking about *that* word.

"Lesbianism." I covered my face with my hands out of embarrassment. I could barely manage to say the word out loud. "Is that what this is? Is that what we are doing together?"

Joanna reached up and pulled my hand away from my face and held onto it. "Hey, Stace, it will be okay. We will stop soon and find a way to get back to being just friends. I promise."

I looked up at her. "But don't you feel major guilt about this? I want to do what God wants, I want to stop . . . but I also really like how it feels." I pulled her into me by her shirt and kissed her lips. I sighed and pulled away as shame rushed in immediately following the excitement of feeling her lips on mine. She never pulled away.

"I don't think I feel the guilt as strongly as you. I think what we share is really special. But yeah, I agree, as Christians we need to do what is right. We have to stop." She pulled me close and I rested my head on her chest. I felt lost and sad.

Later that week we were back at church youth group together, sliding into a back pew a few minutes late. The band was well into a lively version of "I Could Sing of Your Love Forever." I so loved being there with Joanna, in my favorite place. Though I had started to wonder if our sin was more obvious at church.

Calvary Temple was large and warm. The old brick building had lots of expansive rooms, but also lots of small cozy areas with well-worn chairs and smooth wooden pews. My family had grown up there, my friends were all there, my life was there.

I had ambled off to Sunday school there when I was a toddler, earned Crusader badges as a tween, and helped decorate for countless baby and wedding showers in the basement with the old purple carpet. I had laughed and cried and sung my heart out with my friends at this youth group. This was my home.

"Hey, let's go sit with Allie and Lisa over there." I got up to join our other friends, but Joanna grabbed my arm and pulled me back.

"Nah, we're good here."

It was a bit weird, but I settled in next to her for the service anyway. When the music ended, Pastor Gabe got up front to begin his message

"Tonight we're going to talk about something that's pretty taboo. But I think you guys can handle it. I'm talking about homosexuality."

I froze.

Hearing the word *homosexuality* spoken by my pastor, in my youth group, surrounded by my friends made my blood run cold. My legs felt like they were filled with cement, and my heart was overcome with dread.

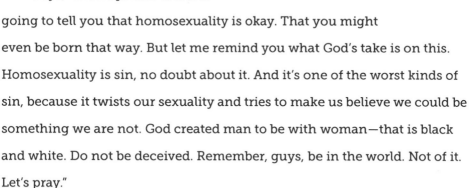

Pastor Gabe sat on a stool at the front, his expression serious.

"Guys, listen up. This world is going to tell you that homosexuality is okay. That you might even be born that way. But let me remind you what God's take is on this. Homosexuality is sin, no doubt about it. And it's one of the worst kinds of sin, because it twists our sexuality and tries to make us believe we could be something we are not. God created man to be with woman—that is black and white. Do not be deceived. Remember, guys, be in the world. Not of it. Let's pray."

There it is.

My worst and deepest fears, *confirmed*.

If my church was saying this—the place I had wholly trusted, the place that had loved me since birth—*then it must be true.*

I stole a look at Joanna, but she ignored my glance and kept a pretty good poker face. I looked around the room to see if any of our friends felt the same horror I felt, but everyone looked calm. They even seemed to be gently nodding in agreement. Even worse. *Do I look too scared? Am I letting anything slip? Is there a spotlight on us?*

Okay, *chill*. No one was looking at us. I was trying not to freak out, but I felt totally gutted.

Homosexuality is the worst kind of sin.

Is that me? Was I the *worst* kind of sinner?

I knew I was a sinner, like we all are, but I thought I was a pretty good person deep down. I always followed the rules. I tried to be kind, thoughtful, and helpful with my friends and my family. Sure, I got impatient sometimes (okay, maybe often) and didn't like to share my favorite chips with Cody. But the worst kind of sinner?

If this is a disease of sin, how and where did I contract it? I was definitely one of those annoying people-pleasing perfectionists. Maybe that was my problem?

Before I met Joanna, I was so focused on not lying or swearing—maybe I didn't see this sin sneaking in the side door. But when? Was it all the church events I went to, or was it all the time I spent in school, listening and earning good grades? My favorite TV shows were *Dr. Quinn: Medicine Woman* and *Touched by an Angel*. I'm pretty sure neither Sully, Michaela, Tess, or Monica ever mentioned homosexuality!

These feelings for Joanna had seriously snuck up on me. I couldn't control them, as much as I tried. I had never felt these desires for boys. The thought of kissing a boy repulsed me.

I closed my eyes.

Something must be really wrong with me.

Chapter 5

Winnipeg, Manitoba

Allie, Lisa, Joanna, and I made our way back through the theater lobby. The smell of popcorn and candy added to my excitement.

"You guys, seriously, didn't you think *Mulan* was beautifully animated?"

Lisa looked toward the ceiling and thought about it. "Yeah, I guess. I totally forgot those were all drawings! Only you think about that stuff, Stace."

Joanna smiled and shook her head. "You and your obsession with animation!" She slung her arm around my shoulder in a jokey "friend" way. I was painfully aware of our friends walking with us and quickly shook free of her arm. I was terrified they would think something of it.

"Yes, I did think about it, and it was gorgeous! Do you guys know how many people and drawings it takes to make that?"

I loved drawing and animation. Had since I was a kid and became fascinated with Disney movies. Every year my family took a road trip to Walt Disney World, where I would revel in all things animation. We drove all the way from Winnipeg to Orlando, Florida, in our motorhome, listening to music and having a great time together. My parents knew I wanted to be an animator, and they encouraged me to follow my dreams. When I was twelve, we got to see the attraction "The Magic of Disney Animation" at MGM Studios. I remember pressing my face up against the glass, watching the animators at work in the large room below. They were drawing characters like Roger Rabbit and Genie from *Aladdin*, with special blue pencils. I couldn't believe they got to draw for a living. One day, if I worked hard

enough, maybe that could be me. I truly believed it was possible. After all, my great-grandmother had been an artist too. It was in my genes.

I stopped daydreaming about animation and snapped back to the present.

"Are you guys ready for grad?" I asked. "Grad" was the big formal dinner and dance for seniors at the end of the school year.

"I can't wait! My mom is going to pick up my dress from the tailor's tomorrow," Allie squealed. "It's too bad you go to a different school, Joanna, otherwise you could come with us. What about you, Stace, are you excited?"

Joanna looked at the ground, her face mopey. "Yeah, too bad."

Oh no. Allie had brought up a sore spot between Joanna and me. There might be another fight later. She didn't like the idea of me going to a fancy dance and maybe dancing with a guy. Or having fun with girls without her. Joanna was so jealous lately, and it was kind of surprising. It actually made me a little bit scared.

"Um, yeah! It will be fun going with you girls! Who needs boys, right?" I felt a pang inside as the truth of that hit close to home. It was so lonely not being able to talk to my friends about what Joanna and I shared behind closed doors.

"Who cares if we don't have dates. We will totally have an awesome time! Get ready!" Lisa did a little dance on the spot, making me laugh. I wanted to stop worrying about how Joanna felt.

Allie nudged me playfully. "What about Doug, Stace? I think he really likes you. I thought he was going to ask you to grad. Do you like him?"

Joanna's stare burned into me. I needed to be careful how I answered this. I hadn't mentioned it to Joanna because I didn't want her to get mad over nothing.

"Who's Doug?" Joanna was ticked.

I shooed her comment away like a fly. "Oh, I think he likes someone else. Anyway, he's not my type. It's gonna be so fun going with you girls—way less stress, right?" I smiled as convincingly as possible, trying not to reveal the tension I felt.

"Yeah, true," Lisa said. "All right, we gotta run. See you Fridaaaaaay!"

Lisa and Allie did another silly dance on the way out of the theater doors, waving goodbye.

I was left to contend with Joanna's questions.

"Why didn't you tell me about Doug? What, do you *like* him?" Joanna was mad. We pulled out of the movie theater parking lot and headed toward her grandma's house.

I was so tired of this pattern. It had been a year of ups and downs. Trying not to kiss, but kissing. Trying not to do more, but failing. On top of that, her obsessive need to keep tabs on me was getting exhausting. I was beginning to feel really trapped, in more ways than one.

"No, of course I don't like him. You know that, Jo." I reached down to grab her hand. I got caught in this cycle a lot. I felt the need to reassure her, but I didn't want to keep encouraging the sexual stuff between us.

She sighed and reluctantly held my hand. "I just don't want to lose you. I know we need to stop what we are doing, but I don't want to lose you."

My thoughts and emotions were so muddled. I kept holding her hand and stared out the window.

The next day I threw my Bible and journal into my backpack and took off on my bike to a picnic table beneath my favorite tree in Assiniboine Park.

35

I was petrified by the magnitude of this struggle. Sometimes the oxygen in my room was not enough and I needed to get outside where the fresh breeze could remind me I was alive.

Christianity. Homosexuality. They do *not* go together, not in the slightest. They do not exist in the same universe. Pastor Gabe preached against homosexuality a couple more times that year, and each time fear took up a larger residence in my heart.

He kept referencing these few verses, and I really needed to study them. I couldn't bring myself to study them in my bedroom where my parents might find out.

1 Corinthians 6:9-11 (NIV)

Or do you not know that wrongdoers will not inherit the kingdom of God? Do not be deceived: Neither the sexually immoral nor idolaters nor adulterers nor men who have sex with men nor thieves nor the greedy nor drunkards nor slanderers nor swindlers will inherit the kingdom of God And that is what some of you were. But you were washed, you were sanctified, you were justified in the name of the Lord Jesus Christ and by the Spirit of our God.

Leviticus 18:22 (NIV)

Do not have sexual relations with a man as one does with a woman; that is detestable.

Romans 1:25-27 (NIV)

They exchanged the truth about God for a lie, and worshiped and served created things rather than the Creator—who is forever praised. Amen.

Because of this, God gave them over to shameful lusts. Even their women exchanged natural sexual relations for unnatural ones. In the same way the men also abandoned natural relations with women and were inflamed with lust for one another. Men committed shameful acts with other men, and received in themselves the due penalty for their error.

I looked up into the clear blue sky, overcome with despair. I wished I could turn this feeling into enough conviction to change my desires, but it only made my shame and fear increase.

I didn't want to go to hell. That was a real, visceral, terrifying possibility. If only I could ask someone at church about these verses. But I knew I couldn't—that would shine a light on my struggle.

I put my headphones on and leaned back against the table. I closed my eyes and let the soothing sounds of the *Contact* movie score calm my nerves. I looked up at my favorite tree, admiring the spectrum of greens. God could hear me better when I was in nature. Or maybe it was that I could hear him better.

God, I don't understand this. Did you make a mistake when you made me? I don't know what I did to have this struggle in my life, but I'm sorry.

Chapter 6

Spring 1998

Winnipeg, Manitoba

Our limo pulled up to the convention center, and Lisa, Allie, and I, in our fancy grad dresses, crawled out carefully. I smoothed the purple crinoline of my gown. I still couldn't believe my mom had sewn this! She had done such an amazing job

"Girls, don't we look fabulous?" Lisa exclaimed as she spun slowly in her emerald green dress.

We entered the large banquet hall with its white-covered tables and huge windows revealing the twinkling lights of downtown Winnipeg. I looked out at the big dance floor, with a disco ball hanging in the center and flashing colored lights onto every surface.

This was the official end of high school. I wasn't sure I was ready for a new chapter yet. All the students from our grade 12 classes were here, and it

hit me how grown up everyone looked in their suits and dresses. I noticed a lot of my girlfriends holding hands with their boyfriends, and I felt jealous. I wished I could have a boyfriend and blend in like them. Actually, I wished I *wanted* a boyfriend. For a second, I wished Joanna could be here, but the thought also scared me. I felt freer away from her lately.

Doug spotted me and crossed the room. He smiled and tried to give me a hug. It was awkward. *Oh no, does he like me?*

"Hey, Stace, you, um, look pretty," he said. Then he looked up quickly and changed the subject. "This place is fancy, hey?"

"Yeah, it's great! Um, I'm going to go take some pictures with Lisa and Allie. I'll see ya later." I needed an excuse to not keep talking. I was scared he might ask me to dance.

The night was full of silly dancing with my girlfriends, and posing for pictures and hugs with almost all of my classmates. Something about finishing high school made everyone feel nostalgic, including me. I successfully avoided any offers to dance with Doug, but by the end of the night, I did miss Joanna. I had told her I would drop by her place afterward so she could see me in my dress.

41

Joanna smiled at me as she opened the door of her grandma's house. "Wow, Stace, you look beautiful!"

I didn't realize how much I had been wanting someone to look at me like that all night. I felt a strange warmth rise up in my body and tried to ignore it. Joanna grabbed my hand and pulled me downstairs and into her bedroom. I knew I shouldn't go. I had told myself I would just stop by and then continue home.

"Thanks. I did miss you tonight. But we had fun dancing."

"Not too much fun, I hope? *Doug* better not have stared at you too long in your dress." She winked, but there was a trace of a threat. She pulled me close. "You wanna stay over tonight? It's so late, you may as well."

Say no. You can do it.

I tried not to look at her. "Don't worry about Doug. I didn't even see him. I'm not sure I should stay, though. I told my parents I would come right home after grad."

"Aww, please? You only just got here." Her hand traveled up to my face and started to pull me in for a kiss. I pulled away at the last second.

"Jo, please. We can't keep doing this. It's wrong."

"I know, I'm sorry. I just . . . love you."

Oh, that was confusing.

I love her too . . . I think. Or maybe I just love what we do together? I'm not sure. I probably won't ever have this with another girl. There's no way I will fall into this sin again.

I sat down on Joanna's bed, my dress crinkling around me.

"I love you too, Jo. We just need to get back to being best friends. It's the right thing, and it's what God wants."

She sat beside me and rested her head on my shoulder. "I know, I know. I just can't help what I feel." She grabbed my arm and pulled me into her. "Stay, please?"

I felt weak.

"Okay, fine. But I should get home early tomorrow. Can you undo the back of my dress so I can change?"

She unzipped me, and I felt her arms sneak inside and around my middle. I wanted to relax into this, but I was fighting. She turned me around and pulled my whole body in for a kiss. This time I didn't stop it. Slowly, she pushed me back onto her bed and started to take my dress off.

I gave in.

Chapter 7

Winnipeg, Manitoba

I was cruising down Portage Avenue in my red Blazer, windows down and *Out of Eden*'s new album blasting out of my speakers. If only I felt as happy as this music.

I needed to end things with Joanna, for good. It had been over two years of this back-and-forth with her. I kept trying to end things, but I always got sucked back in. She kept threatening to tell everyone what we were doing, and that terrified me. I needed help with this. I wanted so badly to be honest with someone. But *who*?

Allie? Lisa? Ashley? They were all Christians, and I doubted they could handle this. Everyone believed homosexuality was at the top of the sin pyramid. I used to think that too. How could my friends look at me as the same Stace after knowing?

I turned up the music even further, trying to drown out my fears. If I kept quiet, this Christian world could remain my safe haven. Did I really want to risk losing that? Maybe if I could get away from Joanna's temptations and keep praying and digging deeper into my Bibles, I would find my way back to the right path.

Okay, I can do this. There's no time like the present, I am going to stop by her place now and end this.

Since moving out of her grandma's house a few months ago, Joanna had been living in an apartment not far from my parents' place. It was both good and bad to have her so close. Now I knocked on her apartment door, trying to hold tight to my resolve. This must have been my twelfth time attempting to end things with her. I was ashamed to admit that to myself. I thought I was strong, but her kiss and the way she touched my body weakened me every time, and she knew it.

I heard footsteps approaching from inside and took a deep breath.

Joanna opened the door in her sweatpants, her hair in a messy bun. She looked so cute, but I had to stop thinking like that. She smiled. "Hi! I thought you were going shopping with your parents today."

"Can we talk?" I said evenly.

She opened the door wider for me to come in. There was a look on her face that said she knew what was coming. It always ended with us in bed, but not this time, I determined.

God, please help me do this.

I walked into Joanna's one-room apartment and sat on the edge of her couch. I didn't want to get comfortable. I avoided looking at her and started talking.

"Look, this totally sucks. But we can't be in each other's lives anymore. It's too hard, we end up sinning too much, we just can't. I can't. I'm sorry, but this is over."

Joanna leaned against her kitchen counter and laughed quietly. There was actually a maniacal edge to it. "Oh, Stace. You could never leave me."

With those words I saw a glimpse of her dark side. The obsessive, forceful manipulation I had felt these last few months flashed in front of my eyes. It angered me. It strengthened my willpower.

I narrowed my eyes. "What do you mean, I could never leave you? You don't own me."

She smiled and went to sit on her bed. "Oh, I know. I just mean I know you so well. You don't have what we share with anyone else, and you never will. You know you need me."

Part of me wondered if she was right, and part of me rose up in righteous anger.

Do it now!

"No. This is done. We are done. Goodbye, Joanna."

I turned to leave, but she jumped in front of me. Somehow in the space of a few seconds she went from laughing to weeping. She was good at flipping her emotions like a light switch.

"Please, Stace. I love you. Don't do this! We can stop, I promise. We can just be friends. No one takes care of you like me! You know that. *Please*, don't do this." She grabbed my hoodie and buried her face in my chest.

Be strong, Stace.

"Joanna, no. I'm sorry, I have to—"

She pulled my face down to kiss me, and I could feel my lips touch the tears on her cheek. It took everything in me to resist and pull away.

"No! I have to go. I'm sorry." I could feel my resolve slowly coming unstuck, like old wallpaper from weary walls. My body would soon ache for the comfort of hers. I forced myself toward the door.

She shouted from behind me, "Fine, then GO! But if you go, I may as well kill myself! But before I do, I will send an email to all our friends, Pastor Gabe, and your parents. I will make sure to tell them what we *really* do at our sleepovers!"

Her threats set off so many alarms inside me. *I don't want her to hurt herself! Do I love her? Why am I doing this?* My life would be over if everyone found out. But . . . I had never made it this far in ending things with her. I could taste freedom. I didn't want to do this again. *Keep going.*

I spoke without turning around. I could hear her sobbing. "I'm sorry, Joanna. Of course, I don't want you to hurt yourself. I don't want you to tell everyone. But I have to end this. I'm sorry."

As I reached for the doorknob, she grabbed my shoulder and violently pulled me back. She pinned me against the closet door. I was genuinely scared. She knew this was for real now, and she was desperate.

"Don't go!" she screamed, tears cascading down her face.

Sobs were rising in my throat too. I was panicking. I had to get out of there. "I'm sorry!" I pushed past her and escaped.

As I ran down the hallway outside her apartment, I tried to calm myself. Behind me, I heard a scream of despair as she kicked her apartment door.

But I was finally *free*.

Before going home, I took a detour to my favorite tree in Assiniboine Park. I was a bundle of nerves after leaving Joanna's and needed the silent comfort of this place to unload my thoughts.

I carried my journal with me constantly, worried about leaving it in my room for anyone to find and read. It was the one place I could be brutally honest with myself, and with God. So now I pulled it out and started to write.

Father, I finally did it. I ended things with Joanna. I'm scared and I feel terrible, but I know it's the right thing. Please watch over her so she doesn't hurt herself. Please help me be strong and set me free from all of this. God, I'm doubting my faith, my worthiness, my ability to be loved, my need to live. If I can't change this, and you can't change this, is there any hope for me? No one else will accept and love me this way.

I looked up and wiped away tears. Leaving Joanna was so hard. Maybe I should take advantage of this courage. Closing my eyes, I knew it was time.

I need to tell Mom and Dad.

Chapter 8

Fall 1999

Winnipeg, Manitoba

I balanced myself on the edge of one of our tall blue wooden stools that lined the side of our kitchen. I could barely sit still. My fear and anxiety were bubbling up and threatening to overflow. My dad was still at work, and my mom and I were chatting. I was distracted with finding the right moment to jump in with this devastating bombshell, without escaping out the window first.

My mom and I were cut from completely different cloth. In a lot of ways, we just weren't programmed to understand each other. We both try, but we had been butting heads more lately. I wished we didn't. I was happiest when I could make her laugh in spite of herself, or when we went shopping or for a long walk in our neighborhood.

The love she had for me ran deep, I knew. But fear of God and the expectation to do what the church said was right also ran deep. She spent a lot of her energy making sure she was steadfast and unmoving in her faith. She believed, no matter what, that you must fear God and do what's right in his eyes. Sometimes I wasn't sure if the love came first, or the fear.

I summoned every fiber of courage I had. There was a pause in our conversation, and I needed to seize the opportunity before it blew away in the wind.

"Hey, Mom, I need to tell you something."

She stopped wiping the counter and looked up hesitantly. She knew nothing easy would follow that sentence. I was the good, solid, reliable Stace. If I had something to tell you, I would just tell you.

"Okay . . ." She hung the dish cloth over the tap, turned to face me, and leaned lightly against the kitchen counter. Her words said go ahead, but her tone and facial expression said no, thank you.

I envisioned myself forging ahead toward the right path. I had finally freed myself from Joanna a couple weeks ago. This was the next step. As uncomfortable as it was, I had to do it. I decided to leave Joanna out of it and just talk about the struggle. *Start small.*

"I—well—the thing is, I might . . . I think I might be struggling with . . . liking g-girls."

I felt my face grow hot, but it seemed even my brown hair must have been turning red, given the sheer embarrassment I was feeling. Shame and fear threatened to take over.

I realized that I had wanted *desperately* to be honest with my mom for some time. This was someone who truly loved me and had been there my whole life. She carried me in her womb for nine months. She had nourished my life so carefully and prayerfully. I just wanted her to really look at me and say, "It's okay, Stace. We will get through this together. I love you."

I held my breath.

She crossed her arms and leaned further back against the kitchen counter. Further away from me. I could see it—I could feel it hanging heavy in the air between us—the shock, the anger. *The disgust.*

I could see it in her face. I knew it. I had literally said the worst sentence I could have ever said. *This sin? No. Absolutely not. Not in our house.*

She looked at me. I could tell it was painful for her to meet my gaze.

Through a thick layer of disbelief, she said, "What do you mean . . . you *like* girls? What does that mean?"

How do I even answer this? "Well, I'm struggling with it. I'm just struggling. But I might find a Christian counselor and get some help to work through it."

"Why would you do that?" she spat.

I felt overwhelmingly unsafe. "Well . . . I think it might help. To talk about it, to try to understand why, and how to get over . . . the struggle."

"Well, I don't want to talk about this again until you are *fixed*."

There it is.

That word was a direct blow to the core of my being. Something lodged in my spirit with that shot at me, and I shifted uncomfortably at the sensation of it.

Fixed.

If my own mother thinks I need fixing, then I must truly be broken.

I looked down at my hands, fiddling nervously, blinking back hot tears of heartbreak.

"I, uhhhh . . . yeah. Okay."

On my bike to escape the hurt, I felt like I was carrying an invisible backpack full of sadness and regret. So much sorrow. I had always made my parents so proud and happy. *How can I do this to them?*

I pedaled onto a hidden path that followed a winding creek. No one was around. I exhaled and let the wind carry away my tears. Why did I feel so much worse after being honest? I thought I was doing the right thing. This only confirmed how big and terrible this sin actually was.

I knew my mom would tell my dad when he got home, and even though I was closer to him, I knew he would agree with my mom on the sin meter. He and I bonded over our favorite pizza, laughing at dumb jokes, and singing to Whitney Houston. We had never talked about *sexuality*. No, I couldn't talk to them about this again.

God, help me. I don't want to give up.

I will make my parents proud. I will get back on the right path.

I will get fixed.

Father, there are so many things I struggle with, and so many times I fail you. I get so frustrated. I just want to be perfect for you and I know I can't be all the time. Things have gotten to be too much lately, and they have to change.

Chapter 9

Fall 1999

"So, tell me, Stacey, what brings you here?"

Joan, the counselor, settled in her chair across from me with a clipboard and pen. Her tidy short haircut, beige sweater, and tan slacks reminded me of so many ladies from Calvary Temple. That did not help. *Is it supposed to feel this awkward? I'm just supposed to flat-out tell her my deepest struggle?*

I looked around the room, trying to find the courage to talk. Her office had sickly purple walls full of framed art and certificates, and yet felt empty somehow. A few plants were placed, somewhat haphazardly, in the corner.

Though my mom hadn't been thrilled when I mentioned Christian counseling in our terrible talk a month ago, I really wanted to understand what had happened with Joanna. Besides, I was nineteen now, and I didn't need her permission. I was still surprised Joanna hadn't followed through with her threats of telling everyone about us. She had tried emailing and calling me, but I managed to ignore them. It was *not* easy.

Deep breath. "Well, I have been struggling . . . with liking girls. With being attracted to them. I got caught up in a sinful relationship with a good friend, but I ended it a while ago. I know it's not what God wants. I just want to know how I got here and how to get over these feelings."

Joan was nodding and writing furiously on her clipboard. *Does she feel disgusted by me, like my mom? She must. I hate this.*

"Okay, Stacey. Let's go back a ways. Tell me about your family."

I began to tell her about my childhood, my brother, and my parents. Cody was a couple years younger than me, and we were pretty close growing up. We seemed to understand each other on a wavelength only siblings can, and always found a way to have fun together. Whether we were in the motorhome counting down the miles to Disney World, escaping to perfect our double-bounce on the trampoline, or making a blanket fort in the living room to watch *Back to the Future.*

My dad and I would have long talks in the car, but it was mostly about movies, the latest Christian music album I had, or another of his classic oldies that he wanted me to hear. He loved being silly and making himself laugh, which made me laugh too. I loved his ability to easily have fun.

My mom was a pillar of leadership in our church and in our family. She was happiest when I followed her rules. There wasn't much room for me to question anything, just to do what was expected. I wanted to make her happy, but it was a lot of pressure, and sometimes I felt suffocated. She

had specific ideas about the kind of
Christian girl I should be growing
up, wearing dresses and making
sure my hair was always curled
and pretty—like hers. I never
stopped to ask myself if I liked
those things, until my struggle
began and dismantled everything
I knew about myself.

I told Joan I wished I felt
closer to my mom, and about
how badly our recent talk had
gone when I tried to open up about my struggle.

She stopped writing and looked up. Her gaze unnerved me.

"Have you thought that maybe you have a deficiency in the relationship
with your mom, and you are looking to fulfill it in other women?"

This suggestion made me feel really uncomfortable.

"I don't know . . ."

She explained. "Often when someone is dealing with same-sex
attractions, it can be traced back to a fractured relationship with their same-
gender parent. Once they understand more about the root of the attraction,
they can reorient themselves."

That didn't resonate. Sure, my mom and I weren't as close as I was with
my dad, but still.

"Now that I have explained more, do you feel as attracted to girls as you did when you came in?"

Do I lie and say no?

I stared at the peach-colored sailboat painting behind her and reminded myself that I had come here to be honest.

"I don't feel any different," I admitted.

"Okay, well, we will keep working on this. I know there is a root to these attractions. While we continue our sessions, I have a suggestion for you," Joan said.

A suggestion already—that's good news! I nodded and forced a small smile. "Sure, what is it?"

"Have you heard of New Direction Ministries?"

I shook my head.

"They are a local Christian organization that helps people with their . . ." She paused to find the right word. "With their struggles with sexual sin. It's run by a wonderful man named Tom. You might want to talk to him. He refers to himself as *ex-gay*."

I winced at hearing the word *gay*. It was such a secular word. I was also reeling a bit from her stating that I struggle with sexual sin. But . . . *ex-gay?* So, this person truly *used to be* gay and was no longer gay?

This must *be it*, I thought. God was leading my next step toward the right path. This man Tom *must* have answers. *Yes*, I thought, *let's talk.*

———

A week later, I went to the little dark office at New Direction Ministries in downtown Winnipeg. Tom sat across from me behind a desk. It felt like the beginning of a very strange interview. There were so many things I wanted to say and ask, but it was difficult to keep telling total strangers about my biggest sin. So I asked about his story first.

"Do you mind telling me how you got here?" I asked.

"Sure. Growing up, I struggled with being attracted to men. I went to Bible college, but my attractions were still there. The church was a really tough place to be, so I left it for a while and joined the gay community. They really accepted me. But I always felt God calling me back, reminding me that being gay was not his plan for me. I've been married now to my wife for a long time and I feel so blessed."

I listened, incredulous. I identified with him so strongly. "But how did your attractions to men go away?"

"It wasn't easy. But I just kept praying. I believed, I trusted, I asked God to take it. I prayed the gay away. I feel so much better now, knowing I am living a life pleasing to him."

Time to be honest.

"I feel like I am just starting on that journey. I am struggling with attractions to women, but I know they are wrong. I want to live a life pleasing to God too."

"You did the right thing coming here. I have a list of books you will probably want to read. This is a tough journey, don't get me wrong. But you can do it with God's help. Don't give in. Just keep praying and believing."

So I hadn't been praying long or hard enough yet. My attractions were still there, even though I wasn't with Joanna anymore. But Tom had done it, so that meant it was possible to pray this away, right? And he seemed to be whole and happy.

I stood up to shake his hand, my head swimming. I wanted to believe these deep attractions inside me could be prayed away, but something inside was resisting. Hopefully the books he gave me would have more answers.

"Thanks for your honesty. I'll keep praying."

He shook my hand and looked into my eyes. Could I sense a deep sadness in his? It bothered my spirit, but I ignored it.

I stepped out onto the sidewalk, blinking in the bright sunlight. I inhaled the crisp fall air. My resolve was renewed.

Maybe I can be ex-gay too.

Chapter 10

Winnipeg, Manitoba

Ugh, these colors don't go to together. This is so frustrating.

I had been in a dark computer lab for a few hours trying to get this brochure design done on time. But suddenly my eyes were pulled off the screen by a figure crossing the lab. My chest filled with a rush of tingling. It was Megyn, one of the instructors in the year-long Graphic Design program at my community college in downtown Winnipeg. I had chosen this program because animation wasn't really taught anywhere, and I loved working with computers. I was a few months in.

I wasn't a student in any of Megyn's classes, but I saw her around a lot. I couldn't help but admire her athletic build, her thick shoulder-length auburn hair, her enticing blue eyes. She drew me in. The pull was overwhelming. This attraction was not helping me walk down the ex-gay path. But I couldn't help it.

I watched her walk over to help one of her students in the lab. She moved with such cool confidence. As she leaned down, her face was lit up by the computer screen. I caught my breath. She was the most beautiful woman I had ever seen. She resembled Jodie Foster, who I'd had a major crush on ever since seeing the movie *Contact*.

When Megyn moved, things seemed to click into slow motion. I was powerless to take my eyes off her. What's worse, there was a rumor going around that she was gay, which only fueled my need to study her.

Afraid she would notice me staring, I forced my eyes back onto my own computer. The thought of her being gay both thrilled and terrified me. Maybe I could find a way to talk to her. She would understand my feelings for other girls. She was so separate from my family and church community, maybe it would be safe.

I struggled with the lid of my coffee cup, trying so hard not to spill. My hands were trembling.

My friend Denise, who worked at the community college, was also friends with Megyn. I had found my way in and had suggested that the three of us go out for coffee. So here we were.

We settled into oversized leather chairs in the corner of the coffee shop. I tried to do my best impression of someone who didn't have insides that felt like Jell-O. The fact that Megyn now knew I existed on this planet made me feel lightheaded.

Denise started the conversation. "So, Stace, how are you liking the classes?"

I took a sip of my mocha and tried to act cool. "Well, I think it's going okay, but those *instructors* are pretty brutal."

When I'm nervous, I make jokes—something I'm always trying to rein in. To my surprise, Megyn laughed. The sound of her laugh was so exhilarating, it made everything in my chest dance.

"Oh, we will try to do better for you then!" Megyn smiled, her gaze fixed on me. I could barely take it. Frantically, I tried to stuff this attraction away, like trying to conceal a giant monster under a tiny bed.

Soon, my anxiety disappeared as conversation flowed easily between the three of us. Both Megyn and Denise were older than me, but now that I was twenty, age didn't seem to matter as much. I kept stealing long looks at Megyn as she spoke. She was so incredible. Being near her felt good. *So good.*

A few weeks later, Megyn and I were walking her dog, hanging out just the two of us. We had gone for coffee on our own a couple times since the first meeting with Denise. Every time I was near Megyn, I felt like I was floating. I would do anything to spend more time with her. I was surprised that she wanted to spend time with me too.

"That place over there makes the best cinnamon buns." Megyn pointed to a charming bakery on the corner of her street, nestled inside a historic brick house.

"Oh, yes please, I love cinnamon buns!" I exclaimed.

None of my church friends or family knew about Megyn. Allie and Lisa had stopped asking me to hang out a while ago. My youth-leader friend Rhonda, from church, had called a couple times asking what I was up to. She had been a mentor of mine, taking groups of us to youth conventions and leading Bible studies. But I didn't want to talk to them. I kept putting them off, saying that I was too busy with college. I knew they would all ask me who I had been hanging around with, and I didn't want to crack open that Pandora's box.

I stared up at the towering elm trees lining Megyn's street, dappling the bright sunshine on the sidewalk. The houses were big and old and had lots of character with their large weather-worn porches, colorful brick exteriors, and tall windows.

"I love this area of town. I would totally live here," I said.

"Yeah, well, tell that to my ex-girlfriend," Megyn said coolly.

My eardrums almost exploded.

I knew by the *way* she said that word that she wasn't talking about a friend, but a relationship. A relationship with another woman. *She was gay.*

I tried to react with indifference, but inside, my heart was having a rousing Mardi Gras. *Oh my word, oh my word, keep cool.*

"Oh, yeah? When did you guys break up?" I asked casually.

"A while ago. But we still share this guy," she said, gesturing to the fluffy little dog in front of us on the sidewalk.

"Oh, I'm sorry." I tried not to sound excited.

"Ah, you know how it goes. Wasn't meant to be. So, what's the plan for you this weekend?"

I was still trying to collect my thoughts. I wondered if her telling me she was gay meant that she could see I was struggling with this too.

"Not too much. Tomorrow I have to work on that assignment for school." I nudged her playfully. "Other than that, just church."

Why did I add that about church?

Why do I feel ashamed about mentioning church?

"Oh, church, hey? Not my thing," she said.

I knew it. Of course, she doesn't go to church. She's gay.

"Yeah, I grew up in church. It's not that bad, actually," I said quickly. I needed to change the subject. "Hey, should we go try one of those cinnamon buns?"

She looked at me and smiled. "You bet!"

It felt fantastic to make her smile.

Megyn and I were out for dinner one night, as we had been doing a lot lately. We had spent a glorious afternoon together perusing a local bookstore. We had sat on the floor, flipping through graphic design books, laughing and critiquing the logos and why we thought they were good or bad. Every time I accidentally (on purpose) brushed against her arm, or felt her leg touch mine, an electric shock shot through my body so palpable I almost jumped in response.

Now as we sat across from each other at the restaurant, I exclaimed, "I'm so glad to have all my graphic design coursework behind me!"

Megyn smiled. "Yeah, I bet. It's a lot to get done in twelve months. Congrats on finishing! I knew you would do well."

As I fiddled with my napkin, I wondered if I could possibly tell her that I have feelings for girls. Not feelings for *her* specifically—no, I would *die* before admitting that. But if I could tell her about my struggle, maybe I wouldn't feel so alone. I shifted nervously in the booth and tried to ignore that the low lighting made everything feel romantic.

I cleared my throat to make sure my voice was still there.

"So . . . how long have you known you were gay?" I asked.

She smiled, pushing aside the dessert menu between us. Her eyes had a calm intelligence that looked right into my soul. It both unnerved me and made me feel unbelievably fantastic. She knew things, about life. Things I wanted to know.

"How long have I known? I guess as long as I can remember." She held my gaze. The air between us felt magnetized. Her face was so alluring it made me dizzy. Surely she could hear my heart beating, since the sound was drowning out everything else in my ears.

"So . . . have you ever wanted to change it?" I managed.

She looked more closely at me and raised one eyebrow. She did this often, and it made my entire body go weak.

"Change it? You mean, have I ever wanted to be straight?" she inquired.

"Yeah . . . I guess." I looked down quickly, wondering if I should not have brought this up.

"No. This is who I am, and I'm pretty happy about it." She kept her eyes on me.

I wanted to yell in response, *Yeah, I'm pretty happy about it too!* Instead, I tore my eyes away from her and stared out the window.

She waited for me to speak. She knew I had something to say. *Just tell her.*

"Yeah, I think I might . . . like girls too," I admitted slowly.

On the word *girls*, I forced myself to look back into her eyes. She was looking back, her face slowly melting into a smile. I didn't see any shock, fear, or disgust.

Wait, was that recognition?

"Really? Hmm," she said softly.

I was overcome with an intoxicating high, now that she knew.

"Yeah, I think I might be—"

"A lesbian?" she helped, one eyebrow up.

I didn't have the courage to say *struggling*. How could I tell her I was trying to be ex-gay? As I sat there across from Megyn, that idea made *no sense* anymore. When I was with her, I forgot everything outside of her orbit.

"Maybe," I admitted.

As dim as the restaurant lighting was, I wished the power would go out completely so I could hide my mix of embarrassment and endorphins.

Megyn smiled and took a sip of her coffee. *She seems pleased with this news. Did she already know?* "Don't worry, Stace. It will get easier to say the word *lesbian* before you know it."

I smiled back, feeling wonderfully fuzzy. *Did Megyn just call me a lesbian?* I couldn't ignore the euphoria rushing through my body.

As we left the restaurant, it felt to me like our friendship had just shifted in a distinct way. I was elated, but down deep, I also felt very torn. Megyn's knowing this fragile piece of me changed things.

Later that night as I started my car, worship music flooded the interior, and with it, intense guilt and shame. The music was like a chorus of reminders that I was ignoring my faith to hang out with Megyn. And now she knew my deepest secret.

I hadn't just admitted my secret to a Christian counselor in an airtight room. I had told someone who likes girls. Someone whom, I had to admit, I was starting to feel real things for.

I closed my eyes at the weight of that. The Christian, ex-gay part of me was so disappointed that I had told her. But the struggling, liking-girls part couldn't *help* but celebrate.

Anyway, what could happen? We were just friends. *She doesn't like me like that. I'm not going to overthink this.*

Father, please help me. I'm starting to have real, deep feelings for Megyn. I love how it feels when we hang out, when we talk, how she understands all these feelings. Help me to figure out how to navigate this, I pray.

Chapter 11

Fall 2002

Winnipeg, Manitoba

"Look, it's snowing!" I exclaimed, gazing out the window of the bookstore where Megyn and I were absorbed in the Art section. "Wow, it's already snowed a lot. We should get going, eh?"

We headed toward my Blazer in the parking lot, big soft flakes falling gently around us. It was dark and silent. The twinkling lights from the surrounding stores made the night feel enchanted.

On a whim, I bent down quickly, scooped up some fresh snow, and threw it at Megyn.

"Hey! No fair!" she laughed, and quickly lobbed a snowball back at me.

Soon we were hiding on either side of my car, trying to pelt each other with piles of soft flakes and laughing with glee.

"All right, all right! Truce!" Megyn put her arms up. "Time to get inside and warm up!"

I unlocked the car and we got in.

I was breathless. Was it from our impromptu snowball fight, or the rush of endorphins from being around Megyn? Suddenly I had the most intense urge to lean over and kiss her. I quickly glanced at her; she was looking at me.

No, Stace, don't do it. Remember Joanna. I fought against it, but it took every fiber of my being. I started the car and drove toward her house.

That was close. I was in *big* trouble.

After dropping Megyn off, I drove home, buzzing from the feeling of being near her. But the further away I got, the more the Christian parts of my life came back into focus. I couldn't ignore this anymore. I felt like I was leading a double life. I was riding a slow-moving train that was quickly gaining speed, leaving behind Christian Central, and heading right into the heart of Lesbian Town.

We had been friends for almost two years now. If we kissed, I would definitely not be able to stop things. Then I would be stuck in sin again, like with Joanna. I had to stop it now, even if that meant throwing myself from this train. I started to panic. It was time for drastic Christian measures.

I knew just who I had to tell—my older friend Rhonda, from church. She wouldn't mince words. She would be brutally honest with me and help me find my way out of this suffocating lesbian fog.

———

Rhonda's house was always comfortable, but in that moment, I was incredibly *un*comfortable. I wrapped my hands around my mug of tea, trying to gain some comfort from the heat. Admitting this to Rhonda wouldn't be easy. She could be blunt and tended to call things as she saw them. But it felt like the best chance to push myself back to the right path."So, what's up, Stace?" She looked at me with a big smile. I really didn't want to disappoint her. We'd known each other for years at Calvary Temple, and I looked up to her. She knew me as the silly one who tried to make people laugh and helped her lead Bible study. Now she searched my face, trying to figure out what was going on.

I had to cut to the chase with her. *Please, God, help me do this.*

"Okay, so here's the thing. I don't know how or why, but I have been struggling with liking girls." I tried to sound calm. I kept my gaze on the floor as I forced the words out. If I looked at Rhonda's face, I knew I wouldn't be able to keep talking. "It's been going on for about five years now, and no one really knows. I've been seeing a Christian counselor. I'm praying all the time and trying to be ex-gay."

Tom, from New Direction Ministries, had been to our young adults group to share his ex-gay testimony, so the term was gaining traction with my church community. However, I'm sure Rhonda never expected it to come out of *my* mouth.

"The reason I wanted to talk to you is because I met an older girl, a gay girl, named Megyn, and we have been hanging out. I shared my struggle with her, and I really like her. Nothing has happened, but I'm scared that something might, so I needed to tell someone."

At this, I finally looked into Rhonda's face. Her eyebrows were raised in shock.

"Okay! Wow. Yeah, that's a lot," she said.

"Yeah. I'm sorry." A blanket of shame enveloped me.

She immediately stood up to grab her Bible and quickly found *them*. Those verses from Pastor Gabe that I had been exhaustively studying for years.

"You know what these say, right?" She spoke directly.

"Yeah, I know. I've been studying them, but like I said, it's been tough."

"But it's pretty black and white. It says homosexuality is wrong." Rhonda was not messing around. Maybe I shouldn't have told her.

"I guess it does. It's just . . . not that easy," I said quietly.

"This is not God's plan for you," Rhonda said seriously.

"I know. I'm sorry." I sank deeper into shame. "I didn't know who to talk to."

"No, that's fine. I'm glad you came. I can definitely help you. I know what you need to do." She sounded sure.

"Okay, great. What?" I asked.

"You need to sit down tonight and write a letter to this Megyn. Tell her sorry, you're not gay, and you can't see her again. That friendship is obviously pulling you away from God, and I'm here to help you cut it off," she said.

That sentence launched a lead balloon in my chest that plummeted to the soles of my feet. *Can't see her again? Cut it off?* Ugh, but what did I *expect* Rhonda to say? This was the absolute *last* thing I wanted to do. It had been almost two glorious years of hanging out with Megyn. I desperately didn't want to let her go.

"I guess . . . I guess that makes sense," I said quietly.

"You agree it's pulling you away from God, right? She is not helping your struggle?" Rhonda's voice got louder.

"No, Megyn's not helping my struggle, for sure," I admitted.

"Okay. Well, then you know what to do." Rhonda clapped her hands together.

Problem solved.

That night I stared at a blank piece of paper, feeling absolute dread. I didn't know what to think or do anymore, but Rhonda's confidence spurred me on. God must be speaking through her, so I just needed to follow through.

I held my breath and mentally applied a thick layer of numbing salve to my feelings for Megyn. I started writing:

m -

I'm sorry if I have given you the wrong idea. But I'm not gay. I'm just struggling with attractions to girls. I plan on getting married to a man once I figure this out, because that's what God wants for me.

I sat there, filling the page with letters making up hollow words the Christian part of me felt I *had* to write. But not ones that were true. Deep down, I realized something tragic.

I had let myself fall in love with her.

All the more reason to end it.

I had to believe that God would reward me for doing this, *the right thing.* This was a massive step toward that right path. One foot in front of the other.

Stace, you can do this.

I pulled up to Megyn's house, clutching my handwritten letter tightly. As I rolled to a stop, I realized my heart was beating so loud I couldn't hear anything else.

Am I about to do the right thing? Or the wrong thing?

No, I need to do this.

Being around Megyn was too mind-boggling. I couldn't keep control, couldn't trust myself. I cared too much, too intensely. I wanted too many romantic things.

I need to cut this off.

I took a deep breath and stepped out onto the crunchy patches of snow that spotted the road. I looked up at the beautiful trees that lined her street, their late fall beauty cheering me on.

Let's do this. Back to the right path.

"Hey, Stace, come on in! I have coffee brewing. How's it going?" Megyn said brightly.

Her light and easy way of being around me tore me apart. I could see how happy she was to see me. It felt amazing. And now, on this perfectly wonderful day, sharing this fuzzy magnetic air, I was going to ruin it.

"Hey . . . yeah, sure, thanks. Yeah, good," I managed.

I was trying so hard to be my cheerful self, but my voice was strained. She must have heard it too. *Do I give her the letter or not?*

Standing in her dizzying presence, I could feel the true weight of this sinking in.

Megyn poured coffee into two mugs and turned back to look at me.

"Hey, you okay?" she asked.

"Yeah . . . yeah," I stammered, avoiding her captivating eyes

Right path, right path, RIGHT PATH . . .

"Yeah, I mean . . ." I forced the words out. "I have this letter for you."

"Oh." Megyn glanced toward the crumply piece of paper in my hand. "Okay, let me get my glasses."

Is that a tinge of excitement in her voice? Does she expect me to confess my true feelings for her? Has she known this whole time?

Suddenly I felt desperate. Why couldn't I have written *that* letter? I knew I had to turn off my emotions in order to move forward.

I followed her down the hallway into her cozy living room flooded with early-afternoon sun. We had spent many hours in here talking, watching movies, sharing meals. It was beginning to feel like a second home to me. This little piece of paper was about to end all that.

I handed her the letter. She looked up at me once more, the beauty of her face taunting me to forget everything.

"I don't have to read this," she said, holding it out in front of her. She could sense my intense anxiety. She was trying to give me a way out.

I wanted to snatch the letter from her and plead, "*No! Please don't read it! It's full of lies! I love you!*" I wanted so badly to grab her, kiss her, and tell her how I felt. But I knew that was the struggle talking.

I have to be strong. I have to.

I heard my voice respond, as if it was coming from outside my body.

"No . . . you have to read it."

"Okay," she said, slowly unfolding the letter.

I wanted to die. I wanted the earth to open and swallow me. This horror was unfolding in slow motion. I studied Megyn's face, like I had done way back in the computer lab. I watched her gorgeous eyes travel back and forth as she read my empty confessions. The lightness and joy drained from her face. I could feel her begin to build up a wall, right in front of me.

Silently, she finished reading, slowly folded the letter, and handed it back to me. Her eyes revealed a deep sense of betrayal.

"You're giving it back to me?" I was numb.

"I don't need it," she said coolly.

That's it. I had broken her trust. I had lied to her. I said I wasn't gay. I had said I wasn't like her.

Am I? Aren't I?

There was nothing more to be said. I grabbed the letter, stood up, and threw it in the garbage. As I walked out of the room, Megyn followed me silently down the hallway. We both knew I needed to leave. This was the last time I would be welcome in her house. I wanted to dig my heels in, kicking and screaming. I was holding back this dam of heartbreak with all my strength, feeling it about to burst any second.

But the hard part was over.

I did what God wanted. I ended it.

My body felt monumentally heavier as I walked back to my car, a dull ache numbing everything. Maybe if I got away from Megyn's house, her enticing world, her intoxicating presence, I would start to feel lighter. As the physical distance between us grew, my heart throbbed painfully. I had to pull over. The ache was overwhelming.

What have I done?

When I finally got home and turned on my computer to check my email, my heart stopped. Megyn's name had popped up.

s -

You'll never know how close you came.

- m

What? Was she admitting we almost had a romantic relationship? Was she admitting she *actually* had feelings . . . for *me*? I was suddenly and completely heartbroken. It was so heavy I could barely breathe.

We almost had something. *And I ended it.*

———

God, help me. This feels like too much. I will keep going if this is the right path, but please . . . help this hurt less. I am being pulled apart from the inside out, and I don't know what to do. I love her, and now . . . she's gone.

———

I deeply grieved the loss of my almost-relationship with Megyn all alone. I was still living at home with my family, but I couldn't tell them what was going on. They had no idea I was going through this, and I needed to keep it that way. Still, being physically close to them brought me some small comfort.

One night, I was watching TV with my parents while Cody was out. He had become pretty popular and went out a lot with his friends. A commercial burst onto the screen advertising Rosie O'Donnell's talk show. I immediately felt myself shrink into the couch. I wanted to hide. Rosie had recently come out as gay, and it was all over the news.

My mom clicked her tongue in disgust when Rosie's face filled the screen. "Ugh, that's just sick," she said. Her tone signified the end of a discussion, not the beginning of one.

They are all sick, was what she meant. The revulsion on her face when I had told her I was attracted to girls flashed in front of my eyes.

I couldn't speak. All I could think about was Joanna and Megyn and this constant struggle to become ex-gay. I was failing, and was so ashamed. God must be as disgusted as my parents.

Somehow, I nodded right along with my parents as if in disbelief at "those gay people" and how they were so lost. Inside, I was screaming for my mom and dad to see me, to understand that I might be one of "those" people. My entire being cried out for comfort and acceptance, but I had nowhere to turn. I was completely alone.

————

"Hey, can we talk?" I was standing in the doorway of Cody's room. He was typing furiously on his computer.

"Oh, yeah, sure! Come in." He saved his document and swiveled around in his desk chair.

I closed his door behind me and flopped onto the bed. This despair over losing Megyn was becoming too much. I needed to talk to someone, and Cody seemed like less of a threat than any of my friends. I didn't care anymore if he knew my struggle. In fact, I wanted him to know.

Even though Cody was younger than me, as we aged we had started to look more the same age. He was tall and thin, and people often mistook him for the older sibling. We looked so much alike, with the same brown hair, brown eyes, and similar glasses.

"Ugh. I just need to talk to someone." I exhaled.

Cody's eyebrows popped up. "Okay, shoot."

"So, Joanna. She and I were more than friends. We . . . dated . . . I guess?

For a couple years, until I could finally cut it off. No one knows. I know God thinks it's wrong. I definitely know Mom and Dad think it's wrong," I confessed.

"Yeah . . . honestly, I had a feeling about you and Joanna. I never liked her, you know. She was obsessed and suffocated you." He shook his head.

My confession didn't seem to faze him at all. His candor was refreshing, and I was so relieved he didn't react in disgust.

"Yeah, it was terrible in the end. And I'm still struggling with being attracted to girls. For the last while, I was hanging out with someone named Megyn. She was an instructor from college. *Ugh*, I totally fell for her. I ended

up telling Rhonda, and she told me to write Megyn a letter to end it. I did that a few weeks ago, but honestly, I can barely function. I am so utterly heartbroken."

I ran my hands through my hair. Cody and I rarely had serious conversations like this. We're not the mushy kind of siblings who share their feelings all the time. We're much better at being silly together. Yet, he sighed in what felt to me like empathy and support. "Man, I'm sorry. If I were you, I couldn't do it. I wouldn't be able to deal with that big of a struggle. That sucks. I'm really sorry."

I took a deep breath. "Yeah, it seriously does."

"I'm sure it will get better with time," he encouraged.

"Thanks. I'll let you get back to it," I said.

I felt a little lighter.

Chapter 12

Winnipeg, Manitoba

"Stace, I want you to meet someone," Rhonda said. We were in the hallway at church, surrounded by our friends. The young-adult service had just ended, and I was catching up with everyone. Luckily for me, Joanna had stopped coming to Calvary Temple. I had taken a break from church too, to spend time with Megyn, but after ending things with her I came back. It was good to be "home," but I felt strangely out of place.

"Oh? Who?"

Rhonda looked excited. She hadn't asked me how I was doing since I gave that letter to Megyn. I wished she would. Even though it was a couple months ago, my heartache was still enormous. But because I knew it was sinful to feel the way I did about Megyn, I didn't feel like I could talk about my grief with Rhonda. All she had done was check in with me to make sure I'd delivered the letter, like it was some errand to run. *Great, that sin is cut off. Next!*

"His name is Justin. I think you guys would really get along," Rhonda said with a grin.

She must think I'm over liking girls, now that I'm not with Megyn anymore, or at least she wanted me to pretend I was. *Now I'm supposed to just date a guy?*

My ongoing prayers for God to take my struggle away felt futile. I still loved Megyn. This anguish was all my fault. I was the one who had pursued that friendship. *That relationship.* I needed to work hard now to get back to the ex-gay path.

Maybe Justin would help.

I took a sip of my iced tea, and tried not to think about escaping the booth Justin and I were sitting in.

"You look beautiful today, Stace." Justin smiled.

He was very good-looking, as far as guys go, with his dark skin, toned muscles, and carefully groomed facial hair. Yet I felt zero attraction, even though we had been dating for almost a month. I hadn't been able to find a reason to say no to going out with him—not a reason I could be honest about. When he came to pick me up for our first date, my parents were over

the moon. That made me so happy. I hadn't seen them smile like that in a long time. So I trusted God to fill in the spaces. I chose to believe that God had brought Justin into my life for a reason.

I forced a smile and thanked him. I was so uncomfortable with his attention. "So," I said, to change the subject, "what's the plan for you this week?"

I felt bad, but as Justin talked, I couldn't even focus on what he was saying. Instead, memories of Megyn and me, and thoughts of what we could have shared, floated by lazily, hitting the inside of my ribs with a sharp pain.

I snapped back to reality when Justin grabbed my hand across the table.

"Earth to Stace, did you hear what I said?" He smiled.

I resisted the strong urge to yank away. My skin crawled when he touched me. I didn't like it at all.

"Oh, sorry, what was that?" I said.

He smiled and pulled at my ring finger. "I said, don't put rings on this finger. You know, for the future."

I wanted to throw myself through the nearest wall. Did he think he was being smooth? My insides twisted with discomfort.

"Oooookay," I said, "let's not get ahead of ourselves." I pulled my hand away and shook it at him teasingly.

God, please change my feelings, or get me out of this.

Two months later, Justin and I were still together. I even threw him a birthday party in my parents' basement. It was quite a lively shindig, considering it was a bunch of church friends and no alcohol. After everyone went home, Justin and I were alone, cleaning up the mess.

"Thanks for throwing me this party, Stace," Justin said as he swept up chip crumbs.

"Yeah, no problem. It was fun," I said, gathering paper cups into a garbage bag.

We'd been dating for three months, and somehow I had avoided kissing him by saying I wanted to "take things slow." But I couldn't keep that up forever.

Some things felt nice, especially if I ignored the numbness in my heart. Making my parents happy by dating a boy filled a huge void. Life was easier when I made them happy, like the old times. Ever since my struggle began with liking girls, I had felt like such a failure. They accepted Justin so fast into our family, inviting him for dinners and game nights, that I didn't want to ruin it.

When Justin and I were out in public, we fit all the typical molds. I didn't have to worry who was around or if they suspected I was sinning. No one thought twice. I could blend in. And I figured it made God happy that I was giving Justin a chance.

But during those moments when I could escape to my favorite tree, I admitted to myself that I was suffocating. My heart hurt. It ached for authenticity. I couldn't keep doing this much longer.

"So, you're sure I can take your Blazer home tonight?" Justin put on his jacket.

"Yeah, definitely. I can get a ride with my parents to church in the morning. Meet you there." I gave him a quick hug goodbye, making sure to avoid his face.

I was getting ready for church the next morning when my cell phone rang.

"Morning, Rhonda. What's up?"

"Hey, Stace, did Justin stay over there last night?" Rhonda sounded a bit exasperated.

"Uh, definitely not." I sensed that something was off. Panic started building in my stomach. "Why?"

"Well, I just talked to his parents on the phone. He didn't come home last night."

"Rhonda. He has my Blazer." There's something about the *way* Rhonda was talking. She knew something.

"I'm sure it's fine," she said, clearly trying really hard not to add to my panic. "I'm sure he'll be at church. See you there."

I hung up. I had a terrible feeling.

My cell phone rang, and I jumped at the sound.

Justin and my Blazer had been missing for three days. I didn't understand why Rhonda or my parents weren't more upset. They just kept saying, "Oh, he'll turn up." Like it was normal for someone to disappear for days at a time. I'm sorry, but he wasn't a time traveler. I was so mad. Somehow, I felt like I was being duped.

It was Rhonda on the phone. "Stace, a friend of Justin's family found him. He was walking down a sidewalk not far from their house."

This wasn't really computing, so I stayed silent, hoping she would say more.

"It turns out, on the way home from your party, he stopped at a bar. He ended up getting drunk and doing some cocaine. He didn't have money to pay for it, so the drug dealers took your Blazer as collateral."

"I'm sorry, *what*? He's into *drugs*?! Did you *know* about this?"

She hesitated. "Yes. But we all thought he was clean. He was doing so well."

I was livid.

"The good news is, Justin's parents bailed him out, paid the debt, and got your Blazer back. They had it cleaned and everything!" Rhonda said brightly.

I was raging mad. But . . . I also felt some relief because now I had a *great* reason to break up with Justin, and it had *nothing* to do with me liking girls.

But later that week, I found myself in a ridiculous conversation with my parents.

"Are you *serious*, you want me to give him another chance?" I paced around the kitchen.

"Stace, just think about it," my mom argued. "Justin really cares for you, and there's lots of Christian help with drug and alcohol addiction."

I couldn't believe what I was hearing. This was *only* because he was a guy—I *knew* it.

"No. I'm not getting involved in that. We were only dating for three months. I'm shocked *you* guys are okay with me getting involved in that! No. We are done."

None of us wanted to say what this was actually about. *I like girls.* I knew I *shouldn't*, but I did. I didn't want to be with a boy. Especially not now.

My mom shook her head and looked at the floor. "Well, I'm just saying, you should pray about it."

Okay, fine. I'll thank God that now that I have tried to date a boy, I know for certain I can't do it.

That night I wrote in my journal:

My mom is so disappointed in me, I can see it in her face. She liked me way better when I was with Justin and everything was picture perfect. Things are so much more difficult than that. I wish she understood.

Why can't it be okay to give my love to a girl? It feels true and real to me— way more than loving a boy. Will this ache for Megyn ever lose its intensity?

Chapter 13

Winnipeg, Manitoba

"All right, Stace, I'll meet you at the mall tomorrow." Rebecca pulled her coat up to her ears and made a funny face. "Geez Louise, it's freezing!"

I laughed. "I know! Why is winter so cold? I'm gonna go before I freeze solid!"

Rebecca was a new friend I'd met at Young Adults Group at church. She was hilarious, and we had a lot of fun laughing together. She had no clue about my struggle, and I had no intention of ruining this friendship by telling her. We were standing outside her house, saying goodbye, when a red Sunfire pulled to a stop nearby.

"Oh, my roommate Tams is home!" Rebecca exclaimed.

I looked over at the girl getting out of her car. She had dark curly hair cut into a stylish fauxhawk and was wearing aviator sunglasses. She bent down to grab a handful of snow and casually wiped it on her windshield. For no reason at all, this impressed me.

"I'm out of windshield-washer fluid," Tams said by way of explanation. She waved coolly and smiled at Rebecca.

I climbed into my own car, not staying to get introduced. "Bye!"

Still, I couldn't help thinking, *Hmm. She's cute.*

A couple weeks later, I was sitting in a pew at church, staring up at the large wooden cross that hung over the pipe organ. I was thinking about Megyn again. It had been six months since I gave her that letter, and I still daydreamed about her. The familiar ache had lodged in a corner of my heart. It seemed to be there to stay. As I saw Lisa approaching me, I quickly shut a trap door over these thoughts.

"Stace, are you coming to the Rebecca St. James concert tomorrow?" she asked.

"Yes, I can't wait! I hope she does stuff from her *Pray* album." Rebecca St. James was so hot with that Aussie accent, but of course I didn't tell Lisa that.

"Cool, I'll save you a seat. I gotta go help the band set up. Talk later!"

Church life used to be all I knew. But now that I was twenty-two, it was harder and harder to find belonging there. I kept praying, I kept trying not to like girls. But I kept *really* liking girls.

I stood up with everyone else and clapped through upbeat versions of "God of Wonders" and "I Have Come to Worship." We came to the part of the service where you introduce yourself to new people. I always want everyone to feel included, so I usually look for the person who is sitting alone and go talk to them. As people started to mill about, I glanced behind me. Amid the crowded pews, two bright, crystal blue eyes caught my attention. The stranger's shy gaze briefly met mine, then darted away, as if she felt uncomfortable at being seen.

Wait, she looks familiar. And she was sitting alone. I'll go talk to her.

As I walked over, I recognized her as that cute girl Tams, Rebecca's roommate. I offered a warm smile.

"Hey, I'm Stacey. Well, my friends call me Stace. I don't think we've met, but I saw you outside Rebecca's a couple weeks ago?"

Up close, her eyes were a startling clear blue. Their beauty took my breath away.

"Hey. I'm Tams."

I could tell that was hard for her, even to say those three words. This gentle soul was not an extrovert. We chatted for a few minutes, me doing most of the talking.

I soon settled back into my pew a few rows in front of her. There was something about her. Intensity and kindness wrapped in a wise, old soul.

I wanted to know more.

Over the next few months, Tams (short for Tammy) became a good friend. Rebecca had a new boyfriend and didn't have much time for either of us, but we were naturally drawn to each other and enjoyed doing things together.

"I'm going to get my usual. What about you, Tams?"

We were sitting at our favorite breakfast spot in Winnipeg, a restaurant called Stella's. I wrapped my hands around my mug of coffee and gazed out

the window at the cloudless blue sky. The prairie winters here are freezing, but at least there's lots of sun.

"I think the scramble this time. Everything here is so good. Maybe I can have a bite of your hash browns?" She smiled at me, revealing her dimples.

"Of course!" I smiled back. I felt so comfortable with her.

Since letting Megyn pull me off the ex-gay path, and Rhonda's reaction reminding me that every Christian would run to the nearest Bible in response to such news, I thought it best to keep my secret from Tams.

"So, tell me about when you and Rebecca went to Bible School in Germany. It sounds so cool! I've never been to Europe but would love to go one day," I said excitedly.

Tams added cream to her coffee. "We were at *Capernwray Bodenseehof*. It was an amazing time. I made a lot of friends. Rebecca is the silliest, as you know. We laughed so much!"

"Oh my word, she is hilarious!" I agreed.

Our food arrived, and as I took a big bite of the warm rye toast covered in delicious homemade jam, I said, "Tell me more about your time at Bible School." I looked into Tams's eyes and tried not to get lost. When she felt safe, she would break out into boisterous laughter, but calm wisdom was also part of her DNA. As I got to know her better, I was finding her beautiful inside and out. But I was not going down *that* path, not again. We were *just friends*. Besides, she was a Christian. She couldn't be gay.

I was safe this time.

Tams and I whizzed down the highway outside Winnipeg toward a little tourist town called Winnipeg Beach. As she drove, I stared out the window, noticing that the snow had begun to melt off the farm fields. We were slowly inching toward spring.

"Thanks for inviting me to your grandma's house," I said. "I am so glad to get out of the city for a little while. I hope it's not too cold so I can do some sketching by the lake."

Tams smiled as she concentrated on the road. "It'll be fun. It's so relaxing there, and my grandma makes the best bread and cinnamon buns."

I threw my hands up in a silly display of excitement. "Oh my word, grandma-made bread *and* cinnamon buns? Stop it!" But Tams seemed to enjoy my enthusiasm over small things, and she smiled. For my part, I enjoyed feeling myself relax a little more into the person I was meant to be, whenever I was around her.

"So, you're really close to your grandma, right?"

"Yeah. She's my favorite person on earth. You'll see why."

As we had gotten to know each other better and Tams had told me more about her relationship with her grandma, her family, and her rough childhood, I began to see a fuller picture behind her self-confidence and independence. I looked over at Tams admiringly. My eyes traveled to her full pink lips. I wondered what it would feel like to kiss them.

Whoa, Stace! Get a grip.

"Come on now! You've got to really get in there!" Tams's grandma stood beside me at the kitchen table, chuckling as I tried pathetically to knead dough for the famous cinnamon rolls. Tams sat across the table from us, smiling at my awkwardness.

When we had first arrived at the little house where she'd lived alone since Tams's grandpa had died, she had opened her door to greet us with a huge smile. She embodied every grandma I would ever want to know. Her short grayish-brown curls, her floral-print muumuu worn over a chunky frame, and her knitted slippers just *invited* you to love her. She grabbed us both, even though she and I had never met, and gave us one of those tight hugs that people give when they don't care about being polite. Those are the hugs that make the world feel okay for a moment.

Now I laughed out loud at the misshapen dough in front of me. "Well, I don't know, can you help me?"

She nudged me gently with her hip so I would move over and shoved her big, weathered hands into the mass. I watched her knead with the ease of what seemed like a thousand years of experience.

"Tams, I thought you were bringing me some help today!" She laughed to herself some more and began to roll out the dough. Clearly, she loved to tease. I had never so quickly felt at home and at ease in a new place and with a new person.

"Sorry, Grandma. I guess Stace won't be having any cinnamon buns later!" Tams smiled at me, her eyes sparkling.

"Oh, come on!" I dropped into a chair as they both had a good-natured laugh at my expense.

That evening we enjoyed a delicious homemade Ukrainian meal of pierogies, cabbage rolls, and kielbasa. Hot coffee and fresh cinnamon buns for dessert, and I decided I would never leave this wonderful place. My stomach and soul were both full and satisfied. After playing a couple rounds of cards and watching some of Grandma's favorite game shows, we all decided to go to bed.

Tams's grandma told us to share her master bedroom, and she would sleep in the guest room. I got changed into my pajamas in the bathroom, and was quickly reminded of the first time I slept with Joanna. *That* would certainly not be happening tonight. Still, I felt a bit nervous. Would it feel strange to share a bed?

Tams and I crawled under her grandma's soft sheets and thick, carefully sewn quilts together. Suddenly, I realized how tired I was.

"I hope this is okay, Stace," said Tams. "I always share a bed with my friends when I bring them to Grandma's." Her voice was soft in the dark room.

"Sure, of course." *Don't be weird, Stace.* I rolled onto my side so my back was to her. Even so, I was aware of her warmth close by. "This bed is so comfy. Thanks for bringing me here. Night, Tams."

She rolled over too and let out a contented sigh. "You're welcome. Night, Stace."

I watched the moonlight stream through the window and listened to Tams's breathing become heavy and even. *This is nice.* I really enjoyed being in bed beside a girl again, but I tried not to overthink it. *Maybe I should tell her about my struggle soon.*

———

Tams and I sat on opposite ends of the small couch in my parents' basement. We had just finished watching *Monsters, Inc.* I loved being around someone who didn't mind my incessant gushing about animated films.

"Seriously, did you notice the details of the character designs, and how unique the monster world was? I just love that movie!" I said passionately.

Tams smiled encouragingly. "Yeah, it's really well done." She never rushed me or made me wonder if what I had said was dumb.

I was still keeping my struggle encased safely inside, as if tied down with thick ropes and fastened with padlocks. But I felt safe with Tams. After sharing the bed at her grandma's, I had started to think I would be comfortable being honest with her soon. Besides, Tams hadn't grown up in a Christian home. She didn't become a Christian until her teens. Maybe she would be less judgmental.

Our conversation changed course gently and naturally, like a small creek winding through the forest. It suddenly felt like a good time to tell her.

I grabbed a nearby pillow and plopped it on my lap for comfort. "Tams, I need to tell you something. Something that I have been struggling with for a long time."

She looked at me intently, revealing her genuine concern. "Sure. What's wrong?"

"I usually don't tell people, especially Christians." I let out a big sigh. "I'm struggling with being attracted to girls. I have been for about six years now. I've been through one rough relationship, and I ended another one before it became sexual. But I fell for her hard, and it still hurts. No one really knows. I'm praying hard to be ex-gay. I'm asking God to change it."

Tams's face didn't change, except to reveal further care and concern. There was no trace of anger or fear. No disgust to be seen. She didn't seem to care where the nearest Bible was. She looked deep into my eyes. "Stace, I'm sorry you've been going through that. It sounds really hard."

The tenderness of her words freed something inside me. Something that had been caged and neglected for way too long. Someone was finally acknowledging how tremendously hard this struggle was. The validation felt incredible—maybe even healing. Tears came to my eyes. I started breaking down. "Yeah . . . yeah, it's been *so* hard."

I was overcome with emotion in Tams's compassionate presence. I hadn't given myself permission to say that out loud before: *This is hard*. Until now, I had only said it was *bad*, and I had been fighting so hard against it.

Tams moved over beside me and gently pulled me in for a hug as I cried. She accepted me, as I was in that moment—struggle and all. Her presence invited my vulnerability and promised to keep it safe. I closed my eyes and leaned into her welcoming embrace. I let her care wash over me.

Finally, I felt a little less alone.

After Tams went home that night, I didn't feel any regret or embarrassment. I felt sweet relief. I drank it in slowly. Our friendship felt sacred, protected. And even if it was a Christian cliché to admit, it felt blessed by God's hand. The genuine love Tams gave me felt like the fresh morning sun, warming my face.

Jesus, thank you for Tams. She and I have become quite close lately, and she has been an amazing support for me in this battle of lesbianism. I pray that we will continue to be a support to each other.

Chapter 14

Spring 2003

Winnipeg, Manitoba

I was in my room practicing Jennifer Knapp's "Martyrs and Thieves" on my guitar. I kept getting tripped up on the chorus. I had only been taking lessons for a month, but I'd wanted to learn for years. My guitar sounded like prayer to me. When I strummed, it quieted the chaos in my head.

Mid-strum, Cody appeared in my open door.

"Hey, got a sec?" he said.

"Yeah, sure." I motioned that he could sit on my bed. "What's up?"

He closed my door and sat down.

"So, remember when you were telling me about Joanna and Megyn?"

"Yeah . . ." *What's this about?*

"Well, you know my friend Eric? He's more than my friend."

Please don't tell me what you are telling me.

"Wait, what?" I tried not to look shocked. *No, not both of us. Please.*

"Eric is my boyfriend. We have been together a while. All my friends know, but obviously Mom and Dad have no idea." Cody's face showed a sort of hardness.

I tried to act cool. "Wow. So, you're dealing with these attractions too?"

"Yeah. I've known since I was five, though. It's been a lot of years for me, too, trying to figure out what God thinks of this." Cody took a deep breath. "But I saw what happened when you tried to tell Mom. I just can't face that kind of rejection—it's too much. I know what they would say. I'm going to wait until I'm financially independent and out of the house to come out."

I tried to take this all in. I needed clarification.

"So, are you struggling with it, or are you saying you're gay?"

"Well, I'm not struggling *anymore*. I'm definitely gay. I tried fighting it for so long, and I tried dating girls. It felt like kissing plastic." His eyes looked tired, like he'd been on an exhausting journey.

I looked down and shined a spot on my guitar. My thoughts were scrambled.

"Well, this is . . . something! I'm still struggling a lot," I said.

"Yeah, I know. And I'm sorry you are. I'm not walking away from my faith, but I'm just tired of struggling. This is who I am. Sorry I never told you earlier, but you know how it is." He smiled weakly.

I couldn't believe I never saw this coming. I hadn't meant to be selfish, but I had been so focused on my own struggle.

"Hey, I'm sorry," I said. "I didn't know. You know I love you?" It felt a bit awkward to say, but I wanted to make sure he knew.

"Yeah, I do. Love you too." He got up and playfully threw a song book at me. "Get back to playing more cheesy songs."

As Cody left, the fire inside of me burned bigger and brighter, as if his news had poured gasoline all over it. I couldn't let my parents down now. They could barely handle *me* struggling with this. How would they handle *both* of us struggling, or one of us—let alone two—*giving in*?

I had to be the one to change. I had always been the sibling who caused less trouble. Cody would run away as a kid, but I never did. He would often get frustrated and argue with Mom and Dad, and I would try to make jokes to ease the tension. I did what I needed to do not to rock the boat. I had to be the good one.

I have to be ex-gay.

In the weeks after I told Tams, whenever we were together, I relished the ability to talk freely and openly with her about my struggle. She was ever so patient, asking me questions about myself, about my faith, about God. She herself didn't quite understand why I was struggling so much with the faith-and-sexuality aspect. She had become a Christian later in her life than I had and didn't carry guilt around the same way I did. We talked a lot about our different experiences with our faith.

"Stace, I just don't understand why you think God thinks being gay is the worst sin. Aren't we all sinners anyway, regardless of who we love?" Tams asked.

"Well, yeah, but I mean, it says it. In the Bible. Which is God's Word. It says homosexuality is wrong."

"Doesn't it also say I shouldn't have short hair or get a tattoo? Or eat shellfish?"

"Yeah . . . but, well, obviously some of those things aren't valid anymore."

"But this one still is?"

"Yeah, I *guess* it is. You're the first Christian I've met who has even hesitated at the thought of it not being the biggest sin."

"Well, the God I met, the God I know—he doesn't really care about that. He just loves me. He just loves *you*."

I wanted that to be true. To the core of my being I wanted it to be that easy. I envied Tams, with her simple faith and her ability to be okay with massive ideas like this. But I'd had years of these messages of guilt and shame. They had weaved an intricate web throughout my mind and heart that I couldn't escape. I had no idea how I was supposed to untangle it. It was just easier to believe what I had been taught—that it was wrong and that I should try to become ex-gay.

Tams listened to my arguments and supported me in my struggle. She didn't try to change the way I felt or the way I saw things. She just encouraged me along the way.

One day, I asked her if she had heard about Exodus International, and she settled back into her chair. "No. What's that?"

I had been doing a lot of research, now that the internet had come into common use. It was much easier to look up "ex-gay" and "Christian + gay" in the privacy of a computer, rather than the publicness of a library.

I discovered Exodus International online. It was a large Christian ministry based in the United States, focused on helping people become ex-gay. New Direction Ministries, where Tom worked, was a smaller Canadian counterpart. There was an annual Exodus International conference coming up soon in California.

What if I went? It would be a huge risk, but maybe I'm ready to take the next step. If I really want to try to be ex-gay, maybe I need to go to the source to get answers.

I told Tams my thoughts, and as always, she listened carefully. Then she said, "If you feel you need to do that, then I will absolutely support you."

Chapter 15

Azusa, California

California was a lot browner than I expected. As I sat on the airplane looking at the landscape below, I wondered why it wasn't lush and green like in every Hollywood movie I'd ever seen.

I couldn't believe I had flown all by myself to attend this ex-gay conference. But it felt like the right next step. Since Cody had come out to me, I felt I needed to amp up my tactics on this ex-gay journey. Even though I had never done *any* trip by myself, I felt ready for this. I was taking a chance and asking God to show up.

I didn't want to tell my parents exactly why I was going, but I had to tell them something since I still lived with them. I murmured to my mom, "This will help me with my struggle," and made sure to include the words "Christian ministry." That was enough to reassure her. I mentioned it to Cody too, and he shrugged. Pretty sure he didn't agree with ex-gay ministries.

After arriving on the college campus where the conference was being held, the first thing I did was find my room. I wheeled my suitcase inside and took a deep breath. Since this was a Christian campus, the rules were that girls roomed with girls and guys roomed with guys. This was supposed to be a conference for people trying to become *ex-gay*. Not sure they had thought *that* one through.

From my suitcase I fished out a crisp new journal to record all my life-changing thoughts and sketches. Secured to the top inside zipper-pocket I discovered a handful of cards tied together. *I didn't pack those.* Wait—had Tams snuck them in? She was so thoughtful.

I grinned at her familiar handwriting on the envelope.

The top card read: "Open this one when you get there."

I ripped it open:

Stace,

I know this is going to be a really tough few days.

But I wanted you to know, I'm thinking of you, and I'm praying for you.

You can do this, I believe in you.

I wrote you a card for each day,

so don't run ahead and open them all at once,

I know you! :)

Be encouraged, my friend. You aren't alone.

Love,

Tams

How did she always know exactly how to encourage me? That card was the emotional push I needed to get out there. I needed to meet people. It was now or never.

The California sun beat down on me as I walked out into the neatly manicured campus. I sat down at an empty table near my dormitory, thankful for the shade from the big umbrella attached to it. I quickly got absorbed in my own thoughts and started writing furiously in my journal.

"Hey."

I squinted into the sun to see a pretty blonde girl standing close to me. The large name tag on a lanyard around her neck announced that she was Kassidy from Texas.

"Oh, hey. Kassidy, is it? How's it going? I'm Stacey."

"Hey, Stacey. Mind if I sit?" She had an obvious Texan accent.

"Sure, of course!" I closed my journal.

When she said my name with her soft drawl, a quiet *ting* rang inside my head. *Oh, I like that.* But right away I cautioned myself: *Okay, calm down, this is the place to learn how to* silence *those* tings.

This whole solo trip to deal with my sexuality was a bit unsettling, and I *was* itchy for someone to navigate the waters with. Since Kassidy was at this conference, maybe she struggled the same way I did.

"So, what brings you here?" she asked, smiling at me.

I wanted to laugh. "Probably the same thing as you?" I smiled back.

I quickly poured out my story. It felt both odd and freeing to share this personal journey with a stranger. Neither of us needed to hide behind our straight Christian masks. This struggle was the only thing we *wanted* to talk about.

I shared with her about growing up in Winnipeg, in a conservative Christian family, and about how the struggle had begun years ago at camp. It felt so good to talk to someone about trying counseling, my messy relationship with Joanna, and how I was heartbroken by Megyn. How I tried dating Justin, but it felt wrong.

"Man, I wish this wasn't *so* hard!" I looked past her toward the mountains beyond.

Kassidy nodded in genuine agreement. "I *know* what you mean. Feels good not to be the only Christian struggling with it, though."

I fiddled with my lanyard. "Yes, that is *so* true! So tell me your story."

She shared her journey of being married to a male pastor but struggling with attraction to women. "I'm hoping to learn how to get rid of these feelings here. I don't think pastor's wives are supposed to like other women!"

We both laughed. Her accent was really endearing.

We decided to walk together over to the auditorium. As we did, she looked over and nudged me playfully, "I've never met a Canadian. Thanks for showing me that y'all don't look like lumberjacks up there!"

I had to laugh. "Oh, you are so welcome. But I *do* like plaid!"

She laughed. It was nice to make a friend. It also felt strangely exposing to be so vulnerable with someone I just met.

I looked at Kassidy and smiled nervously as we found a row to sit in.

"There are a lot more people here than I thought there'd be, hey?" I said quietly.

"Yeah, *hey*." She leaned over and jabbed my shoulder gently. "You are so Canadian."

"Oh, sorry, *y'all!*'" I laughed and shook my head. "You're so Texan!"

Kassidy leaned in closer to whisper in my ear. "I didn't really think I'd be attracted to girls while I am here. Did you think about that?"

I was not sure how to respond. As I watched the huge auditorium fill with people wearing lanyards, I could almost feel everyone else's struggles bumping up against mine. It was heavy and uncomfortable.

"No," I whispered back. "I didn't really think about it. Is there anyone specific you're talking about?"

She looked into my eyes. "Yeah . . . you."

Shoot.

The next day, Kassidy and I were sitting at the campus coffee shop with a few other girls we had met. That morning's keynote speaker had invited people to breakout into small groups to share their stories of hardship and struggle.

One of the girls, Heidi, had a story similar to mine. She was really struggling here but was trying to make jokes about it. "So, are we calling this *ex-gay camp?*"

Everyone laughed. Kassidy made eye contact with me as she chuckled and stirred her cappuccino. I was so distracted. Knowing Kassidy was attracted to me, seeing it in her eyes and her body language, fed something inside me. Something I loved but that I was also desperately trying to turn off. I mean, *come on.* I found her attractive too, but we were at an *ex-gay conference, for crying out loud.*

I could feel myself splitting, like when I was with Megyn.

Half of me wanted to numb myself to Kassidy's attention and learn what I had come here to learn: how *not* to be attracted to girls. The other half wanted to grab Kassidy's hand and see where our mutual attraction might

lead. I couldn't deny that I had missed another girl's touch remarkably since being with Joanna. Touching myself did not cut it.

As our group walked over to the next workshop, I told myself not to sit beside Kassidy. But she snuck in and made sure to snag a seat beside me. I was torn—both agonized and thrilled.

As Melissa, the speaker for this workshop, took her place at the front of the packed room, I tried my best to ignore the flirtatious energy beside me.

"Good afternoon, everyone! I hope you all have been enjoying the conference so far, and are getting excited about what God is doing in this place. First let's pray that God would open our hearts to the message of this workshop."

Everyone bowed their heads, including me. Suddenly I felt sheer panic. *What am I doing here? Do I really want to walk away from my feelings and experiences?* For the first time, I was scared that God might *actually* change me.

God, please show me what you want for me.

Melissa was wearing a floral summer dress, but she didn't seem comfortable in it. I wondered what she would rather wear. She began by telling us her story of how she used to identify as a lesbian, but now considered herself straight. I listened very closely.

"Once I started to have same-sex attractions, and even act on them, I said to myself: I must be gay. I *chose* that identity. But that is not *God's* identity for me." She gestured toward heaven, and a chorus of *amens* rose out of the crowd. She spoke with confidence, but I sensed a sadness too.

"We must focus on God, not overcoming homosexuality. God wants us to refocus on him, and choose our identity *in him*. Don't focus on changing the behaviors or the feelings—but change your *identity*. *Choose* to change your identity, and God will help the feelings and behaviors change over time."

This was unsettling. How much time? I had given it over six years now. I wanted to believe Melissa and celebrate alongside her, but something inside prevented me.

"Guys, let me tell you. I remember saying to my gay friends, 'I don't know about you, but I'm 99.9 percent gay.' I am here today because God was that 0.1 percent and he took over!" Her voice got louder and more passionate at the end. There were even louder *amens* in response.

I needed a break.

Standing in the sunshine with Kassidy and our other new friends, I took a deep breath. I wasn't sure what to think.

Kassidy sidled up to me. "Hey, Canada, wanna go chat?"

I needed a distraction, and she was a pretty great one. I tried not to smile at the nickname she had given me. "Yes, please."

We broke off from the group and walked a ways together in silence. I wondered if she, too, was feeling confused by the instructions on how to be ex-gay. I wondered if, like me, she was even still *wanting* to be ex-gay. We found an isolated table near a little waterfall that fed into a rocky pond.

"Oh, this table's got *ambiance*!" Kassidy said as we settled into chairs opposite each other.

She's right, I thought. I wasn't sure if that was a good thing.

We talked through what we had learned from Melissa in the workshop. It didn't seem to resonate with her either, since she had struggled with same-sex attractions her whole life. I wanted to shift the conversation a bit

"So, how's it going with those attractions? Anyone else catch your eye?" I smiled and avoided looking at her while I watched the water.

She laughed gently. It sounded sexy. "No. I'm just *really* attracted to you." She paused. "Actually . . . I'm totally *enamored* with you."

I lost my breath, the same way I had when Joanna first kissed me. Hearing those words spoken softly and with her accent was intoxicating. I welcomed it, like a salve over the questions burning in my heart.

"Oh. Well, okay then . . ." I kept my gaze on the pond. There was a charged silence between us until I could look at her.

"I feel something too." I was oddly aware of hearing my own voice and that it sounded . . . *sensual?* When did I learn to flirt?

We continued talking, but most of the communication was with our eyes. We had clicked into full-flirtation mode. It was exhilarating to be caught up in this circular force of attraction. I had never had the chance to truly flirt, intentionally, with another girl before. I'm sure I flirted with Megyn, but I wasn't fully aware. Sitting there now, feeling high off the continual dose of lust and endorphins, I was *oh*, so aware.

We realized that it was getting late and people would wonder where we were, so we headed back. As we walked side by side, I was entirely preoccupied knowing that if I stopped and kissed her, she would kiss me back.

This is so incredibly conflicting.

This was not why I had come here. And yet, something about the intensity of this conference was creating an immediate intimacy with these people I had just met. With Kassidy. We were so outside of normal life and reality and could finally just be ourselves. It was the only place I had ever felt this free.

That night, I lay in bed, exhausted. The euphoria had calmed once I was away from Kassidy. I couldn't keep doing this emotional and spiritual up and down.

As I prayed, I felt the truest part of me softly cry out. In the solace of the darkness, I needed to confess something.

God, I don't feel like this ex-gay path is the right path for me. I'm so sorry. Help me see what the right path is.

I felt God say to me, "If I came to bring life, and life more abundantly, is this what that looks and feels like?"

No.

This ex-gay life *wasn't* the abundant life I wanted. But it seemed to be my only option.

I fell asleep floating in a sea of restlessness.

Chapter 16

Summer 2003

Azusa, California

The next morning I emerged from the dormitory into the now-familiar California heat. Kassidy was sitting at the table where we had first met. I felt a rush of excitement.

It was my turn to approach her at the table. "Hey, Kass."

She smiled. "Hey, Canada. Want to sit?"

I sat down opposite her. We looked at each other, saying nothing and everything, getting dizzy off the endorphins. I had to look away.

"So, today is the last day, eh? Guess what tomorrow is?" I said.

"I don't know. What's tomorrow?"

"My birthday." I smiled.

"Oh, wow! Why didn't you say something earlier? We've gotta go out to celebrate!"

"Okay, sure." I couldn't help but enjoy the pull of her gaze. This energy we shared was so heady. If things kept progressing, I wouldn't be able to stop. I didn't *want* to stop. It was a good thing we would be parting ways soon.

A couple of our friends passed by the table.

"Do y'all want to go out tonight to celebrate Stacey's birthday? It's tomorrow!" Kassidy said with a smile.

When the last session ended, a group of us headed to the parking lot to carpool out for a late dinner. I tried so hard to let God speak to me during that last session, but my questions and confusions were too loud and I disengaged. I just wanted to go and have some fun before going home.

We piled into Heidi's little car and sped off toward a cluster of restaurants not far from campus. I sat in the backseat squished between Kassidy and another friend, watching the palm trees whiz by. Having Kassidy's body pressed up against mine made me feel dizzy. As the campus disappeared from view and the conference seemed to slip away, my restraint began to weaken.

This feels good. My leg against her leg, my arm touching hers. I closed my eyes to my internal struggle as Patty Griffin's "Tony" blasted through the car stereo. I had never heard her voice before, but she sang like she was celebrating my temporary liberation. I vowed to enjoy the night.

We enjoyed lots of rousing conversation at dinner. I had never heard the word *masturbation* so much in my life. My friends were clearly growing tired of the struggle too, but didn't seem to know what to do next any better than I did. We needed the release of this outing. It felt good to be ourselves for one evening away from the conference—to be our *gay* selves. Kassidy and I enjoyed stealing long glances at each other across the table and silently communicating in a way that was now familiar.

The lights twinkled around us as we walked back to the car, a mix of emotions swimming in the air. It was well past midnight, and in about four hours the shuttle would come get me for the airport. I had a feeling I wouldn't be getting any sleep that night.

Kassidy gently grabbed me around the shoulders and pulled me beside her.

She whispered into my ear, "I just want you to know—you're getting a kiss tonight."

I lost my breath.

It had been a torturous hour since Kassidy whispered those words into my ear. I was packing my bags and preparing to leave. My roommate had already left, leaving me alone with these intoxicating thoughts.

I heard a soft knock at the door, and suddenly, there she was, standing in my room. Just the two of us. Throughout the conference, we had never let ourselves be alone in a room. With a bed.

I sat on my bed and laughed nervously. "So, this has been an interesting few days, eh?" I took a deep breath and let my body fall gently backward. I was open to whatever happened next.

"Ha, yeah. Yeeeeahhhh . . ." She sat down beside me. Her leg brushed mine and the feeling reverberated through my body. She hesitated a moment, and then slowly lay down beside me.

We both stared at the ceiling, until finally, I propped myself up on my elbow and faced her. I knew what was coming, but I wanted her to make the first move.

She looked into my eyes and smiled. "Happy birthday, Stacey."

At the sound of her silky voice saying my name, I held my breath. We stared at each other. Time stopped. We both knew everything had been building to this moment.

She reached up and gently pulled my face to hers. Our lips touched. We began to kiss, that powerful spinning in my chest returning. We kissed slowly and softly at first. I was totally lost in it. But soon we devoured each other. *Oh, I have missed this.* Why did it have to feel so *incredibly* good to kiss a girl?

At last we tore our lips away from each other, and I rested my forehead on her shoulder. I felt numb and breathless. My pulse was blazing, and I wanted more, but I waited for her cue.

"I can't do this," Kassidy whispered.

Suddenly, she got up and left the room.

In a state of shock, I sat up, still catching my breath. I was alone again. I stared at the floor, then covered my face with my hands. My confusing emotions came crashing down around me. I began to cry as all of my guilt and shame flooded back in.

God, I'm sorry I'm so weak. I can't do this.

As I flew home, I tried to process everything that had happened. I felt more exhausted and confused than when I had arrived.

Whatever Kassidy and I had shared, we left it on that campus. I was infatuated, but I didn't truly know her. I journaled madly, trying to release this turbulence from my heart and head.

I didn't believe in being ex-gay anymore. If this conference couldn't change me, nothing could. *So now what?*

So many questions swirled inside me: How could God love me if I couldn't change? Did I have to walk away from God in order to be in a real relationship with another girl? Being Christian *and* gay wasn't possible, but I didn't *want* to be Christian and celibate. Leaving Christianity to be gay felt about as possible as removing my shadow. God was an integral part of my being, wound up in my DNA, so that was not an option.

Where does this leave me?

I sat there, unable to function. Unable to feel happy. I felt like a 300-pound weight was on top of me.

God, forgive me. I don't think I can change.

Chapter 17

Winnipeg, Manitoba

I was exhausted and bleary-eyed from lack of sleep, but I could see it a mile away in my parents' faces. They smiled and waved on the other side of baggage claim as I wheeled my luggage toward them. They oozed happiness and relief. They thought I was finally and permanently *fixed*. They gave me big hugs, but their joy mixed with my despair and created a heavy ache in my body.

We piled into our car and talked about how hot California was. I didn't want to talk about anything else that happened there. Good thing today was my birthday, a distraction.

"Happy birthday, Stace! I can't believe you're twenty-three! Where has the time gone?" My mom spoke excitedly from the front passenger seat.

I was so lonely. I stared out at the familiar Winnipeg streets as we made our way home. "I don't know. I feel old, I guess!" I tried to force the cheerful tone that always made them happy.

I just wanted to see Tams. She would understand.

We had some birthday cake at home with Cody, and I appreciated that my parents were trying. I knew they loved me. But I wished they knew the *real* me, the struggling me. Would they still love me if they did?

I finally escaped to see Tams and pulled my Blazer up to the little house she had started renting recently with her brother, Mike. When she opened her door and saw my expression, she quietly pulled me inside and gave me a big, warm hug. This was her way of asking how it went. I just held on, not knowing what to say. I rested there, against her strong frame, our spirits communing together. I felt so heavyhearted.

And still *so* attracted to girls.

———

"Does this look right?"

I turned my sketchbook toward Tams, showing her my sketch of driftwood. We were sitting on thick beach towels on the warm shore at Winnipeg Beach. It had been a week of chaos as I unpacked not only my luggage but also what had happened at Exodus and my life-altering doubts about becoming ex-gay. She was the only one I could talk to about all of this.

Tams had suggested we relax at her grandma's for a couple days. Now as I sat there next to Tams, listening to the lapping of the lake and sketching in the sun, I felt so content.

She smiled at my drawing. "Looks awesome. I love the shading."

I continued sketching. "Like I was saying . . . I can't believe how easy it was to flirt with Kassidy. I got totally lost in it."

"Hmm." Tams's response was short, but that wasn't abnormal.

I continued, "And that kiss . . ." I fanned myself with my hand. "Man, was it good! Why does it have to feel so amazing? It would be easier to resist if it was just *fine.*"

"Yeah." Her tone sounded a bit off. I looked over at her. Arms around her knees, Tams was staring out into the lake.

"Hey, everything okay? I know I've been blabbing a lot since I got back."

She looked over at me and then back at the water. Her eyes were troubled.

"I need to talk to you." There was weight to her words that I hadn't heard before.

I closed my sketchbook and turned to face her. "What's up?" I sensed it was something big, but I had no idea what.

Tams looked down, tracing patterns in the sand with her fingers. She opened her mouth to speak, then lost her nerve and closed it. She tried again.

"While you were away at Exodus . . ." She trailed off, losing confidence. This was really hard for her. I started to worry.

"Hey, did something happen while I was gone? Are you okay?"

A small smile flashed across her face. "No, I'm okay. It's just hard, what I have to say."

"Okay. There's no rush. Just tell me whenever you're ready."

She looked up at me, a gentle breeze rustling her thick curls. "I don't know how to say this."

I was truly at a loss. I waited.

"While you were away . . . I realized . . . I realized I have feelings for you. As more than just a friend."

Whoa, what? Wait—is Tams gay? In that moment, my mind flipped back through all our conversations from the past year. She never really talked about boys, but she never talked about girls either. And since she was Christian, I had just assumed she was straight.

"Oh! Okay. *Wow* . . ." I stammered, trying to process this new information.

Tams continued, avoiding my eyes. "I'm sorry. Because I know I'm your only Christian support in fighting against *this struggle*. I don't want t o pull you away from God. I agonized over telling you the whole time you were gone."

At that, her magnificent blue eyes met mine.

"I don't want to lose your friendship. I have never felt this way for anyone before. But I think I'm falling in love with you."

At those words, my soul *tinged*—the loudest *ting* I had ever felt. It leapt with joy

We both sat there, looking out into the lake, letting the dust settle around this weighty confession. I didn't know what to say.

What does this mean for us? What do I do?

I knew one thing for sure. My love for Tams was something I did not struggle with. It was built on the most genuine friendship . . . but beyond that?

Was this my cue to cut and run before the sin started, like I did with Megyn? This felt so different. My friendship and love for Tams was more significant than what Megan and I had shared. Tams and I had connected deeply over our faith. And it was not just an intense infatuation, like with Kassidy. It was so pure. I couldn't just leave.

And I couldn't turn it off.

———

My breaststrokes cut through the tepid chlorinated water at Sargent Park Pool. It was late evening and I had gone swimming to clear my head. With each stroke I vacillated back and forth. *Yes, no, yes, no, yes, no, yes . . .*

It had been a couple days since our conversation by the lake. I was still processing Tams's huge confession. My head was a blur of arguments and prayers. My love for her felt free and real and authentic.

Is this what sin feels like?

I was standing on a precipice, unsure of how to continue. Should I let myself see what would happen if our friendship went further? Could I really do that? *This is the exact opposite direction of ex-gay.* But . . . if I didn't believe in that anymore, maybe it was worth exploring?

As I pushed my body through the water, it hit me.

There was no way I could resist this.

This was a wave that I just had to jump onto and ride.

I got out of the pool and drove directly to Tams's house. Adrenaline was racing through my body as fast as the thoughts through my mind.

She opened the door, surprised to see me standing there with my hair all messy and wet, my jogging pants hastily pulled on over my swimsuit.

I stepped in and closed the door behind me. Our bodies were inches from each other. My pulse was racing, anticipation building.

Looking deeply into her eyes, I could see she was trying to figure out what was happening. I began to let go of the struggle for the first time.

"I think we need to do this."

I pulled her whole body into me, and our lips touched. I felt a rush of both lust and love. This was new. This was *strong*.

Our bodies fit together perfectly, pressed against one another like puzzle pieces. I felt hesitation in her lips as we began to kiss, but she soon gave into it and let it take on a life of its own. It was intense. Electric passion

flowed between us. This felt *unimaginably* fantastic. I tasted the chlorine I had brought from the pool now on both our lips.

We tightened our arms around each other in a way we never had before. I felt in my bones that this new intimacy was just the beginning. Our bodies remained entwined as we stumbled into her bedroom and closed the door.

As we crawled onto Tams's bed, a sense of euphoria took over my entire body. As I pulled her onto me, I was overcome by a feeling that dragged me away at light speed, and I was happily powerless against it.

———

God, Tams and I have started sleeping together. The first time was last week. It was amazing, and those heavy guilt emotions did not flow in afterwards like they did with Joanna. But I know it's wrong. I know this can't continue. Please forgive me. But why does some sin feel so much like real love?

Chapter 18

Summer 2004

Winnipeg, Manitoba

"One quick kiss before we go in?" I smiled mischievously at Tams.

We were sitting in my Blazer in the far corner of the church parking lot. Tams flashed her dimpled smile at me and I grabbed her face and pulled it in for a kiss. We had kept our dating closeted for almost a year, and I was getting very good at knowing when no one was around.

We got out of the car, making sure to walk appropriately far apart to appear friend-like as we made our way into church. Pastor Gabe had started his own church, Soul Sanctuary, not long ago, bringing with him most of us from his young-adult group. It had a more modern and youthful feel than Calvary Temple, but I was keenly aware that any hint of homosexuality within these walls was not safe.

This relationship with Tams was exhilarating, but it did complicate life. Now there were two of us hiding in this closet. From my parents. From Rebecca, Allie, Lisa, Rhonda, and our whole church community.

As we grabbed seats near the back and the worship band started, I felt the familiar pang of my soul splitting in two. I hated being forced to exist as two people. *Straight-single-Christian* Stace, and *gay-dating-Tams-trying-to-be-Christian* Stace.

I was losing track of who I was.

My parents arrived not long after us and sat down beside Tams and me. They had started attending Soul Sanctuary not long after we did.

"Morning, Stace! Hi, Tams!" My mom tapped my knee and leaned over to smile at Tams. My body tensed.

My family life had felt lighter and happier since my return from Exodus. My parents believed I was *fixed*, and now they also knew and loved Tams. As my best friend. What would happen if they ever found out about us? They would never forgive me for giving in to this grotesque sin. I felt the anxiety building in my stomach, slowly crawling up my throat. It lived there a lot now.

I smiled at Mom and Dad and tried to calm my nerves. *Can they tell I slept with Tams last night?*

My mom's smile was the largest in church. She was at her happiest when things *appeared* to be perfect. Her daughter was straight and attending the church she approved of. Life was grand.

I tried to sing along with the worship band, but the noise inside my head was much too loud.

"How was class today, Tams?" I smiled widely as she opened the passenger door.

She climbed in, and I drove toward her place. Tams was attending Herzing College to complete a program in graphic design. She used to work at a photography company hand-painting retouches, and was loving learning how to do it digitally.

"It was good. Photoshop is pretty overwhelming. There's so much to learn!" She smiled, but I could hear in her voice that she was tired. College can be tough on introverts.

She reached over to hold my hand gently while I drove. It centered us both.

"Stace, do you mind if we stop at the store to get some groceries before going home? I want to make you and Mike a nice dinner."

I smiled and changed lanes. "I will never say no to your amazing cooking!"

Soon we were perusing the Mexican food aisle. As Tams was searching for just the right salsa, Janet Jackson's "When I Think of You" started playing on the store's audio system.

"Uh oh, I love this song! Sorry!" I broke out in a ridiculous little dance and started to lip-sync the words, moving between Tams and the shelves of salsa.

Tams tried not to smile but couldn't help it. "Oh my word!" She embarrassed easily, but also loved it when I embraced the silliness in myself. She held that tension so well.

I didn't see anyone around, so I shimmied up to her body, using some intimate hip movements. I wrapped my arms around her middle and kissed her on the neck, then released her quickly. Sometimes I just wanted to enjoy a fleeting moment of what it felt like to be a dating couple in public.

She blushed, grinned, and grabbed the salsa. I admired her dimples all the way to the cashier.

We were chatting and enjoying our taco feast later that night when Tams's phone rang. Mike had brought his dinner into his room to watch wrestling, so it was just us.

"Hey, Brynn, how are you?" said Tams.

I wondered why our friend from church was calling. She and Tams didn't talk often on the phone. When Tams's face dissolved into concern as she listened, I began to worry.

"Okay, well, I'll email her. Sure, let's do coffee tomorrow."

Tams hung up, *not* happy. She let out a frustrated sigh.

"What was *that* about?"

"Tessa, Brynn's friend. She called Brynn. She saw us at the grocery store. She wants to know *what is up*." Tams's face was set—strong and protective. Of me. Of us. She couldn't stand church gossip.

I knew immediately. My dance. There was no way you could dance up to someone like that if they were *just a friend*. Also, there was kissing. *How could I have let my guard down like that?*

My face must have turned white because Tams came to sit close, wrapping her steady arm around my middle. The warmth spread through me and relaxed the tension in my stomach.

"Hey. Stace. Don't worry. I'm going to talk to Brynn. I know she cares about us. I'll be honest and ask her not to say anything. As for Tessa, I'll send her an email and ask her to mind her own damn business."

I was scared, but it was so nice to feel protected.

I was not alone.

Father, I'm sorry, but I love Tams. Is feeling safe and being loved what it looks like to let sin into my life? I just don't understand. I'm so tired of this. How will I ever be able to love a man the way that I love Tams? I'm sorry. I hope after this I can live a life that makes you proud.

Chapter 19

Spring 2005

Winnipeg, Manitoba

"Ugh, Tams, can you look at this? I feel like the perspective is off."

I was sitting on Tams's worn easy chair in her small living room. Holding up a large sketchbook in front of me, I squinted as I tried to see my drawing from another angle. This was the last piece needed for my portfolio to apply to Sheridan College. I loved working in graphic design, but it had been almost five years. I didn't want to give up on my animation dream. Sheridan College had one of the top animation programs in North America, but it was extremely tough to get into. It was also across the country in Oakville, Ontario.

I could feel my perfectionism mingling with the stress of getting this done on time, and my frustration was mounting. Tams's reassurance could always turn down the temperature on my rising panic.

She tilted her head, looking at my sketch.

"Stace, I think it's great. Maybe just tighten up those lines, but I think you are almost there." She rubbed my shoulder in encouragement.

I felt better. I wished I felt more confident about my own skills. Getting into Sheridan would be an impossibly huge step toward my dream of working as an animator. I just wasn't sure I was good enough.

Tams returned to the kitchen to prep veggies for dinner, and I returned to my sketch. She paused in her slicing and dicing and looked over at me from the counter.

"Babe, can I ask you something?" Her tone was serious.

I stopped sketching and looked over at her. "Yeah, of course."

"What are your thoughts on gay marriage?" She held her gaze on me.

We had been dating, closeted, for almost two years now. My questions and feelings of guilt constantly dragged behind us. I was so tired of hiding who we were outside of her little house. We both were. But I felt I had no choice.

I tried to ignore the sinking feeling in my stomach. "Gay marriage? I don't know . . ." I looked around the room, searching for answers. Hopelessness began to creep in. "If I believed God celebrated gay relationships, then I could believe in gay marriage. I'm so far from believing that, though." I sighed heavily.

She returned to chopping carrots. "Yeah, I know. I was just . . . curious." I could hear distant longing in her voice.

I watched her move around the kitchen and wished I could give her more hope. "I'm sorry, Tams. I love you."

"I know. It's okay. I love you, too."

I didn't understand this authentic and unmoving love Tams had for me. She believed in us, in a way that allowed me to explore every dark and scary corner and still land back in her arms. I needed to do my best to never let go of it.

God, I feel so broken today. It's been a while since I wrote to you. I give you my relationship with Tams. I know we need to stop. But it feels pure and real. How I long to have a godly marriage and family, but I have zero attraction for men. Give me strength to move forward

---

We were sitting in my Blazer, parked near Tams's school. I was holding an unopened letter from Sheridan College.

I closed my eyes and shoved it into Tams's hands. "You open it!"

I kept my eyes closed and heard the ripping of paper. There was a moment of torturous silence.

"You got in." Tams's quiet voice was a mix of pride and sorrow.

"What?!" I grabbed the letter from her, barely believing the words in black and white in front of me.

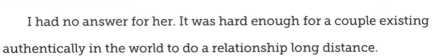

I got in?!

I have to move there?

I have to leave Tams?

Tears escaped Tams's eyes. "I'm sorry. I'm so proud of you. But what does this mean for us? Four years apart? How will we do that?"

I had no answer for her. It was hard enough for a couple existing authentically in the world to do a relationship long distance.

People didn't even know we were together.

We lay breathless, our bodies intertwined beneath Tams's soft plaid sheets.

I was leaving for Sheridan in one week. We were trying to cherish as many intimate moments together as possible. I moved my head to rest in the crook of her arm as our breathing regulated. Buried under the layers of guilt and shame, I sometimes felt like *these* were the moments that felt the most spiritual.

I stared up at the ceiling and silently prayed:

God, are you here in this moment with us? Or are you standing outside the door, simply because we are two women in love, instead of a man and a woman?

The rawest, most tender part of me—the part of my soul that used to be a floating idea—sometimes felt God's grace resting close by. Just waiting. Quietly encouraging.

Other times I heard only deafening silence.

Fall 2005

My mom and I wheeled our carry-ons toward the long line at security. We were at Winnipeg International Airport, about to board a flight to Toronto and my new adventure at Sheridan College. It was really nice of her to come and help me get settled, but I wished Tams was coming with me instead.

Tams and my dad followed us through the airport to say goodbye. I could hear them laughing as they walked, about something silly my dad had said. They had a similar sense of humor. It made me happy, while also leaving me with a deep ache. I wished my parents knew and accepted who she was to me.

We stopped near the back of the line and turned to give hugs. I was feeling so many huge emotions, but I had no idea how to process them. How could I say goodbye to my best friend, my rock, my anchor—also my secret girlfriend—in *front* of my parents? I felt myself shutting down.

I caught Tams's eyes quickly, and we desperately communicated the same message: *This is horrible.*

I wrapped my arms around my dad and felt emotion tap me on the shoulder for a totally different reason.

"Love you, Dad. I will see you soon, don't worry!" I forced my voice to sound strong.

I could see he was fighting back tears too. "Love you. See you soon." His voice wavered.

My mom hugged my dad goodbye, and I could sense she was ready to go through security. I know she didn't think I needed to hug Tams goodbye. Ever since my confession, she was easily annoyed and highly critical of any contact I had with another girl. I knew she was wondering why Tams had even needed to come to the airport.

"Okay, bye, Tams." I put on a smile while holding back every ounce of emotion I had. I quickly gave her a stiff friend hug. This was torture.

Don't kiss her. Don't say "I love you."

I felt her body trembling in our embrace. This wasn't fair.

"Good luck, Stace." I could hear the emotion in her voice. She was fighting too.

I knew my mom's eyes were on us.

"Okay, Stace, let's get going," she said evenly and turned to my dad. "See you soon. Love you, hon."

I didn't dare look back at Tams as I turned to join my mom.

My heart was breaking.

———————

Oakville, Ontario

"I'm going to get my fave, barbecue chicken pizza. What about you, Mom?" I said.

She and I were at a pizza restaurant near Sheridan College. She had been with me for a few days now, helping me get settled. While I attended school, I would be living with an old friend, Maria, and her family from Calvary Temple, who had moved to Ontario a few years ago. It was nice to have a familiar face in the midst of so much change.

We ordered, and then I caught her up on my first day of orientation at Sheridan. There were a lot of fun things to share, but I was hurting inside over missing Tams. I hadn't been able to call her since arriving because I had been with my mom constantly. I was too exhausted to have to answer Mom's questions as to why I would need to talk to Tams so soon.

I had managed to send her a quick email and ask how she was doing. I knew it was tough for her, not to be able to talk to anyone about us. I felt like

I had left part of my body in Winnipeg. But while my mom was with me, I needed to pretend I was intact.

"You have a lot of work ahead, hey? Tell me about it," Mom said.

"Yes, oh my word. Let me get my class list, and I can tell you how busy I am about to get!"

I pulled a handful of orientation papers from my backpack and tossed them on the table between us. I dug around for a pen.

My mom pulled at a card sticking out from the middle of the pile.

"What's this?" Her annoyed tone made the hair on the back of my neck stand up.

I hadn't realized that a card Tams had sent with me was mixed in with the papers. While I was relieved it wasn't one of our "sexy" cards, it was still not ideal. A cartoon elephant was suspended in the air by a huge balloon that read, "Need a hug?"

I braced myself. *Act casual.*

"Oh, that's from Tams. She knew it would be lonely starting Sheridan, so she gave me this card." I grabbed it and quickly shoved it back in my backpack. *I wish I could start this meal over.*

My mom was not impressed.

"Well. That's nice, but you don't need a hug, do you? You are fine, and you will see her at Christmas," she said curtly.

All the emotion and shame and embarrassment and stress I had been holding back was about to burst out. Her response made me feel even more lonely and ashamed. I couldn't keep up this facade, I needed a release.

"Oh, I know. It's fine. I have to use the washroom. Be right back."

I hurried to the bathroom and was immediately grateful to see that all the stalls were empty. I went to the farthest one, sat down, and released huge, wracking sobs. I couldn't even control them. I was surprised at how raw I sounded. They echoed strangely off the deep red stall walls. I hadn't cried in so long. It was too painful.

My mom didn't see me.

She didn't want to.

She never would.

The only person who had ever truly seen me was in Winnipeg.

I was so weak to this sin.

I am alone in this again.

Chapter 20

Fall 2005–Summer 2007

Oakville, Ontario

My heart was pounding with nervous excitement. I had almost gotten lost three times because the Toronto streets were so confusing to navigate. But I had made it to the massive Toronto Pearson Airport, about 50 kilometers from Oakville, and was staring at the empty baggage claim. Tams's plane would be arriving any minute.

I cannot wait to see Tams.

We had both agreed we couldn't wait any longer, so she booked a flight to come visit me over Thanksgiving in mid-October. It had only been about six weeks since that awful goodbye at the Winnipeg airport, but it felt like an eternity.

Finally, people started pouring into the vast room. I spotted her familiar dark curls from far away. I wished the velvet crowd-control rope wasn't here

so I could run right to her. She grabbed her bag and wheeled it in my direction. My heart leapt. Distance *does* make the heart grow fonder.

When Tams spotted me, her face broke into a rare toothy grin. I could feel her energy even though we were still many meters apart.

She rushed into my arms.

My body and spirit needed this so badly. Suddenly my heart was calm again. Before I could stop myself, I pulled her lips onto mine and gave her a huge kiss. We were across the country, after all. *Who cares.*

I looked square into those spectacular blue eyes and smiled. "Hey, you."

Her dimples revealed her joy and she pulled me in again for a hug.

We headed toward the car and Maria's family's house. On the long drive, we caught up on my overwhelming classes, her school finishing up, life in Winnipeg, and the anguish of being apart.

I tried to remember which highway was best and changed lanes. "I can't wait for you to meet my new friend Anna. She's like my little sister. You will love her! We stress about the same stuff, like our drawings and assignments, so we are able to help each other."

Tams reached over and grabbed my free hand. I had seriously missed her calming presence. I felt her looking at me.

"That's great, Stace. I missed you," she said.

I smiled broadly. "I missed you more."

Before getting too close to Maria's house, we pulled over into an empty parking lot and made out for a few minutes. *Man, I have missed these lips. This spinning feeling.*

Maria and her family were Christians and would definitely align with my parents' beliefs—no homosexuality, thank you. We would have to put our "friend" hats on as soon as we walked in the door, so we needed to work off some of this girlfriend energy, *fast.*

As we walked into Maria's house, I quickly hid my feelings for Tams away.

We ran into Maria in the hallway. "Hey, Stace! Oh hi, you must be Tams!" They gave each other a quick hug. I always worried that my friends from church might have a sixth sense about the people I was secretly sleeping with, but all seemed fine.

"Hi! Thanks for letting me stay here for Thanksgiving." Tams smiled.

"Sure, anytime! I'll let you get settled." Maria continued up the stairs.

Tams followed me to my makeshift bedroom in the basement. It was cozy but dark, with only one small window at the far end. Maria's parents had put up temporary curtains to give some privacy between my "bedroom" and the communal stairs. It did the job.

Pulling the curtain closed behind us, I could finally embrace Tams the way I wanted. We tried not to laugh loudly as we fell backward onto my bed to get reacquainted before dinner.

—

Spring 2006

Several months later, at the beginning of spring semester, Tams came out to visit me again. Anna, Tams, and I were piled into the little Mazda I had bought since coming to Sheridan. "Anna, tell Tams about your mark in storyboarding class," I urged.

Flowers were starting to bloom around campus, and the air was fragrant and fresh. Tams had just picked up Anna and me from class and we were heading to get some coffee to fuel us through prep for our next assignment.

Anna laughed modestly from the back seat. "Ooh, well, I got a 94%!"

I chimed in quickly. "Such an amazing job, Anna! I sketched those great scenes from Hitchcock's *North by Northwest*," I told Tams.

Tams paid for the coffees at the drive-through window. "Great job, guys. Good thing you have each other to study with."

"I know!" Anna and I said in unison, and then laughed.

We were giddy from the constant coursework and too much coffee. College was all encompassing, the classes were hard, and we drew nonstop. I was not only trying to keep my self-doubt at bay; I was also working hard to remain tightly closeted. I couldn't deal with my sexuality *and* succeed at Sheridan.

Anna took a sip of her drink. "Tams, what are you working on right now?"

"I have some freelance work for a client in Toronto. I'm designing new brochures and business cards for them, so it worked out really well that I could come stay with Stace for a while."

"Yes, that's great!" Anna grabbed my shoulder from the back seat. "Stace, how are we going to prep for that life drawing exam tomorrow?"

"Let's get back to my place and we'll go over those diagrams, okay?"

She shook her fists in the air. "Yes, pleeeease!"

It felt great to have a close friend here, but I *so* wished I could be honest with Anna. Tams had been staying with me for a month or so, as my "best friend." I couldn't believe we had been secretly dating for almost three years. In private was the only place we had freedom, but lately, even that was making me feel chaotic.

How was I supposed to be a good student, a good Christian, and a good girlfriend all at the same time?

I didn't know where I stood with God, or myself, anymore.

It was all too exhausting.

———

God, please forgive me for letting sin rule my life when it comes to my struggle with lesbianism. So much of me wants to give in and live openly as a lesbian. But for what? The touch of another woman? The kiss of another woman? Is that really what you want for me? Please, show me how to REALLY live for you.

———

Summer 2007

A year later, during the summer between my second and third years at Sheridan, I went home to Winnipeg to try to sort things out with Tams. I was twenty-seven. She and I had been dating for four years, and I was at a breaking point. I couldn't live this dual life anymore. I was beyond tired.

One beautiful summer day, I went to Tams's to try to talk to her. I knew I had to be brutally honest. I looked out her window at the gentle breeze tossing the leaves of the nearby trees. It looked so peaceful, but I felt nothing. I was completely numb. Everything had suddenly become too big.

"I'm sorry, Tams. I can't do this anymore. It's been four years of us being together, hiding, and my prayers are not being answered. I am allowing myself to live in this sin, and that must be why God isn't giving me peace. All I feel inside is turmoil."

Tams sat on the floor, leaning against her bed. Her eyes were red with tears.

"Please, Stace, just talk to me. We can work through this." She let out a huge sigh of exhaustion. "I love you."

I didn't know what to do. A numb, emotionless feeling was fighting to take control.

I looked down and ran my hands through my hair. I was vacillating between throwing a rage tantrum and collapsing in sobs. Instead of doing either, my numbness hardened.

I grabbed my backpack and started shoving into it things of mine that were lying around Tams's house. A couple worn hoodies. Some CDs. My headphones. An animation book I was reading. The sketchbook she had recently bought me. My pajamas.

Tams's sniffling grew louder. She didn't move. She was familiar with my ups and downs and knew I needed to ride them out on my own. Her love was gentle and kind, and always waited for me to come back to it. This time, I just didn't know if I could.

I walked to her front door and stopped with my hand on the knob. I couldn't look back at her.

"I'm so sorry, Tams. Please believe me that I do love you. I just need some . . . time."

I made my way down the steps of her little house, cursing the warm summer air for its false sense of comfort.

———

Jesus, can I ask you to be in the center of this storm? Please be with Tams. Please be with me. I know you are beside us, holding our hands, but please also hold our hearts. This is so freaking hard. It feels so right to be with her. It feels so good. I love her so much. But I can't be gay and Christian. Please surround Tams's and my hurting hearts tonight.

Chapter 21

Spring and Summer 2008

Oakville, Ontario

Cody's name popped up on my phone as I finished getting changed.

After class that morning, I had spent a good hour working out at the campus gym. It had become a beloved necessity in my routine, outside of drawing. Sweating was cathartic, the only way I could quiet some of the noise inside myself. And I was proud of myself for not letting the muscular college jocks intimidate me from lifting weights. Chubby teenage me would never have had the confidence.

"Hey, Cody! How's it going?" I said, happy to hear from him.

"Hey, how's school? You must be close to finishing third year, right?" He didn't sound totally like himself.

"Yeah, we are working on our group films. Agh, so much work," I responded briefly. But since I could tell by his tone that there was a specific reason for this call, I quickly shifted the focus back to him. "What's up?"

"I need to tell you something." I heard frustration in his voice.

What's this about? "Yeah, shoot."

"I wrote a letter to Mom and Dad, and I just gave it to them. I wanted to tell you what it said before you heard it from them. I finally told them I'm gay, that Eric and I have been together for years, and that we are getting married in August."

Wait—married?

GAY married??

I tried to process this news. I had figured he would eventually come out, but getting *married* on top of it really threw me off. The thought of Mom and Dad getting this news was terrifying.

"I . . . okaaaaaay . . ." I stammered.

"Sorry, I know it's a lot. It's been an emotionally exhausting few weeks, and I'm just done." He sounded tired.

"Yeah, I bet. For sure." I cleared my throat and forced myself to be the supportive big sister. "Look, I'm sorry it's been so hard. I'm here for you. It's not going to go well when Mom and Dad read the letter, hey?"

"Yeah, duh. I bet Mom won't even read it. I'm probably going to have to call her and just yell it over the phone." His patience was wearing thin. He was probably right. Denial was a very close friend of hers.

Cody continued. "Anyway, I just wanted you to hear it from me. You'll be at the wedding, right?"

I —gay wedding . . .

"Of course, wouldn't miss it for the world," I said.

"'Kay, awesome. Anyway, good luck getting your projects done. Love you."

The beep that ended our conversation echoed in the empty locker room. I sat down slowly on a bench. So many thoughts were battling for my attention. Something inside of me was groaning under the pressure of trying to hold it together. With that phone conversation, I felt it snap. This news crossed the line.

Cody was *out* and getting *gay-married*.

This would devastate my parents.

I *really* had no choice now. I could never come out and get gay-married, even if I wanted to. Over the last few months, since I left Tams's house in the summer, we had had many hard conversations. I just couldn't seem to live without her in my life. The love we shared was so strong. We had decided to continue our relationship, which was easier for me with the geographical distance between us—me still at Sheridan, and

Tams still in Winnipeg. I could try to just focus on college. But Cody's news brought the sky crashing down around me.

There was absolutely *no way* my parents could handle the weight and shame of *both* of their good, Christian kids . . . gay.

Or gay-married.

I can't do this.

I avoided talking to my parents for a long time and didn't go home to visit them after my third year at Sheridan. It was like waiting for a bomb to drop, wondering when my parents would find out about Cody and if they would want to talk to me about it. The guilt and shame I felt about my relationship with Tams was threatening to crush me.

Tams and I had now been dating for five tumultuous years. I was tired of living a double life. I didn't know what to think anymore. I wasn't even sure if God was there. I couldn't let Tams go, but I couldn't embrace being gay and Christian, so I kept landing agonizingly in the middle.

I had been able to compartmentalize the struggle while at school in order to do well and complete my projects, but it wasn't easy. Years of trying to change something with no results had left cracks and scars on my heart. If I was honest, I felt myself crumbling. This wouldn't be sustainable much longer.

East Aurora, New York

Thankfully, I had an escape. I landed a position as Content Art Intern at Fisher-Price in East Aurora, New York, for the summer. It was far enough away from my parents and Tams that they wouldn't be able to visit me. I could easily avoid any hard conversations or decisions about those relationships this summer. It was also going to be incredibly fun to learn about making toys and put all that I'd learned about drawing so far at Sheridan to use.

When I arrived, I rolled down my windows and drove through the picturesque town.

Colorful little houses with manicured lawns and quaint shops lined the main street. As I drove around town with my windows down, I breathed in the fragrance of summer blooms in the warm air.

I pulled into a parking spot and made my way to Human Resources for first-day orientation.

This is going to be a fantastic summer.

As the summer wore on, I dove into my work and tried to block everything else out. I enjoyed the creative projects and the people I got to work with. But every time I came home to my apartment, my struggles would crash back into view. I avoided calling Tams, and I didn't answer when she called me. I avoided calling my parents. And yet I couldn't stop thinking about them. Cody and Eric were getting married at the end of the summer and I wondered how my parents were handling the news. Had they even read the letter Cody sent them yet?

One afternoon after a long, stress-relieving bike ride, my phone buzzed. It was my mom.

Oh no.

This was unavoidable, so I should get it over with. My stomach flooded with anxiety and I braced myself.

"Hey, Mom, how's it going?" I said breezily.

"Hi, Stace. Well, we just wanted to know if you heard Cody's news." I knew that tone. This was not good.

I tried to sound indifferent. "Yes, he called and told me."

"Well, did you talk any sense to him?" Her tone was angry and disgusted, gaining traction with every syllable. My spirit curled inward to protect myself from it. "We have to tell him he can't do this, we have to get him on our side! We need to be praying for him so he sees how wrong this is!"

Oh, that's right. She believed I was *fixed.* That I was straight. That I was *on their side.*

What do I say? How do I do this?

I can't do this.

I summoned all my courage. "Well, I think this is who he is, Mom."

She exhaled loudly. "That can't be. This is perverted, this is wrong. We need to help him see that. We all need to help him! You aren't going to the *wedding,* are you?" She spat out the word as if it brought a horrid taste to her mouth.

I was panicking, fighting to switch off any and all buttons connected to feeling anything.

"I think I need to support my brother, so, yes, I will be at the wedding," I said. I heard myself talking, but I couldn't feel anything.

Mom scoffed in frustration. "Well, God won't be happy with you if you go. As Christians, we just can*not* support this kind of thing."

I needed to end this phone call.

"I'm sorry, Mom. I'll talk to you later. Bye." I hung up.

Only one thing floated to the surface above the numbness. *I have to end things with Tams for good.*

The chaos inside me wasn't going away. *Just admit it, Stace.* I would never feel at peace about this, and I couldn't keep dragging her along this broken road. I couldn't add to my parents' pile of disgrace. Maybe my only way to peace was to be on my own with God, and not keep living in this sin.

I'm done fighting.

This was a breaking point for me. I had been pretty disconnected already, but after that phone call with my mom I completely distanced myself from anyone who made me feel anything: Tams, my friends in Winnipeg, my friends from Sheridan. All of this was too much. It was too hard to feel. I ignored Tams's calls and texts until I couldn't anymore.

I was outside at a small park near my apartment one Sunday afternoon, sitting and sketching at a picnic table. No one was around and I relished in the solitude. I was trying to relax, and usually sketching helped, but not today. My body was buzzing with anxiety. I scribbled over my drawing in frustration and took a deep breath. I was mad. Mad at myself for not knowing what to do next. Mad at the numbness and chaos inside. Just plain mad at life itself.

My phone vibrated and it was Tams. Again. *Alright, fine, let's get this over with.* I knew it would be easier to break up with her while I was feeling angry, rather than feeling sad and lonely. Sadness was too painful.

I opened my flip phone. "Hey Tams." I said numbly.

"Stace! I've been trying to call you for so long. Are you okay?" She sounded worried and exhausted.

Stay the course, Stace. Don't let her get to you. You know you have to do this for her own good.

"Yeah. Sorry. Look—we need to talk." I said quickly, before I could chicken out.

"Okay . . ." Tams said quietly. I could almost feel her bracing herself over the phone. This was not new territory for us.

A fresh wave of resentment washed over me. *I hate that I'm always the bad guy in our relationship.*

"I can't do this anymore. Cody and Eric are getting married in a few weeks, Mom and Dad are beyond heartbroken. All I feel is chaos, all the time. There's no way I can be gay and Christian and I hate it!" My voice steadily rose in frustration. "I'm sorry I've been avoiding talking to you. But we can't do this anymore. You deserve better. We have to break up, Tams."

I hated how those words sounded, coming out of my mouth. But there was no going back now.

There was silence on the other end. I knew she was trying not to let me hear her crying. *I can't sit here and listen to her cry, it's too much.*

"Tams, did you hear me? We have to break up!" The more the sadness threatened to show itself, the larger the anger grew to overshadow it. I hated this version of myself.

"Yes! I hear you." She managed through sobs. "But Stace, look at all we've been through! Look at how far God has brought us. Can't we just trust—"

I couldn't continue listening to her soft voice pull at my heart. I had to interrupt her. "No Tams, I can't anymore!" I got up from the picnic table and paced nearby.

I need to end this conversation.

"I'm sorry, but we are over. I have to go."

I forced myself to flip the phone closed before she could say anything more. I immediately felt sick to my stomach. I knew I wasn't being fair or kind, but I didn't have enough energy to care. I was in survival mode.

I walked back over to the picnic table and slammed my fists down in rage. My phone flew out of my hand and skipped onto the grass.

Well you did it, Stace.

You finally ended it.

Chapter 22

Winnipeg, Manitoba

I smiled in spite of myself as I looked around the expansive and perfectly decorated back yard. Large, manicured trees and colorful flowers led the way up to the broad patio where Cody and Eric would say their vows. Like them, it was all very classy.

It was a wonderfully hot Winnipeg summer day, with a cloudless sky and a gentle breeze. The ideal day for a wedding.

Scanning the yard, I searched the faces of the people talking in small groups, drinks in hand. I knew Tams was coming, and I was nervous to see her. We hadn't talked in over five weeks.

I had successfully completed my internship at Fisher-Price and had flown home for the wedding. I knew it would be tough for Cody, since our parents and the majority of our extended family wouldn't be there. I was happy to be there for him, even if I was unsure where I stood on the idea of gay marriage.

I saw some old friends and headed over to catch up. On my way over, Cody jumped in to give me a hug.

"Hi, sisterrrrrr!" Clearly, he had had a couple glasses of wine to calm his nerves. I loved it when he was silly and happy. I saw a lightness in him that hadn't been there before he came out.

"Hi, are you nervous? Oh, you look so nice!" I brushed my hand over the front of his crisp blue suit and straightened his bright orange tie. He was the best dresser I knew.

"Thanks! No, I'm not nervous. I'm good!" He smiled and held up his wine. "Thanks for coming, though." I knew what he meant with those words. It must be so hard to celebrate when most of our family had chosen not to celebrate with him.

"I'm so happy to be here. Okay, go mingle!" I gave him another hug, and as he turned to walk away, my eyes caught a glimpse of those familiar black faux-hawk curls.

She's here.

Tams walked up to me slowly, hesitantly. She looked lovely in her black pinstriped pants and white blouse. I tried not to feel a longing.

"Hey." She stood beside me and looked into my eyes. She was a sea of sadness.

I couldn't hold her gaze. I felt such guilt for how I had ended things. "Hey. You look really nice."

"Thanks. You too," she said quietly.

We stood in silence for a moment, not knowing how to navigate this, then moved to find seats for the ceremony. I felt grateful for the distraction so we didn't have to find the words. I think she did, too.

As I watched Cody say his vows to the love of his life, I realized he was truly happy. He smiled like he was finally free. I wanted that, too. But what

would that look like for me? I didn't know. I saw happiness in front of me that I wanted to celebrate, but I felt a deep sadness sitting beside me. The pandemonium continued in my heart. It was a very heavy tension to hold.

After the ceremony ended and everyone applauded Cody and Eric into matrimony, I joined them for some family photos. There was lots of laughter, especially when Cody and I hit our silliest moment and made everyone indulge us for our classic photo pose—the "Chomiak leg lift." It was so ridiculous, but it made us laugh, so for years we had done it every chance we got. He grabbed my shoulder and lifted his leg up for me to hold, and we both grinned.

As the evening wore on and the drinks ran out, I realized how exhausted I was after my quick transition of finishing up at Fisher-Price and getting back here in time for the wedding. I only had a few days before I had to leave again to begin my final year at Sheridan and the scariest project of all—our thesis animated films.

I needed some comfort. I looked at Tams, who was standing beside me.

"Hey, Tams? Would you mind if I came over tonight, just to sleep? I don't feel like going to Mom and Dad's. They won't be happy today, and I don't have the energy to answer all their questions."

She was looking down, but I saw a sad smile escape. "Yeah, sure. Of course."

Part of me wished she wasn't so kind, when I had been so unkind to her. But I was also grateful for it. We said our goodbyes to the happy couple and headed to her place.

Back in her comfortable little house, a wave of emotions hit me. But the wave hit my wall of numbness, and I didn't let it break through. I held strong. It was easier not to feel at all than to feel the vastness of this.

We changed and settled into her familiar bed, but this time as friends. I was reminded of the first time, years ago, sharing a bed with her at her grandma's. My back to her, I felt a hint of comfort at her warm presence. But mostly, I felt terrible about hurting her and not having any real answers.

Her love was the last thing I heard, gently calling to me in the dark of night, as I let myself drift off to sleep.

Chapter 23

Fall 2008 - Spring 2009

Oakville, Ontario

I smiled at my paper as I sketched. *I think Bentley the Bug is finally starting to show himself.* I often struggled to translate what was inside my head through my pencil, but the moments when it clicked were wonderful.

"How's this, Anna?" I held my drawing up for her to see. She was sketching beside me in our fourth-year animation studio on campus. The room was full of nervous excitement, largely fueled by energy drinks.

She smiled. "Ooh, cute, Stace! He's going to be so fun to animate!"

We were a couple months into our final year, and I was working on the character designs for my thesis film. I had been stressing over what to do ever since my first week at Sheridan, when they had told us that everything hinged on our films. If they were done well, it could mean a ticket to a job.

The idea for my film had come to me from a story I heard while with my grandparents. When I was growing up, they had a small cottage near Kenora, Ontario, not far from Winnipeg. Even now, it was still one of my most favorite places on earth. I loved the sweet smell of the trees, the wind on my face in my grandpa's boat, the bouncy, affectionate laughter of my grandma when Grandpa made a lame joke. Their cottage was tiny, but always cozy, and filled with the glorious smells of Grandma's cooking.

One day we had been in the little living room, Grandma rocking in her creaky chair and Grandpa engrossed in his book about war planes. A friend of theirs dropped by and told us about growing up on a farm. He said he used to play violin, and his favorite place to practice was up in the barn loft. That was a stunning visual to me.

Now I was attempting to translate it into my thesis film entitled *Tah-Dah*. Farmer Henry is in his barn loft, trying to play the cello. He's having trouble hitting the right notes, and they fall flat to the ground. A small bug named Bentley, also living in the loft, decides to help Henry, and they make beautiful music together.

That is—they *would*, if I could design all the characters, props, and backgrounds, animate and paint everything, and finish on time. *Cue anxiety.*

My mind boarded an express train for Stress Land at the sheer thought of the amount of work ahead of me

I wish I could call Tams. She always calms me down.

Since I had seen her at Cody's wedding a couple months ago, we hadn't talked. I needed space to focus on my film, and I knew she was still heartbroken over how I had ended things. I was living pretty permanently in my shell of numbness now to protect myself from feeling. Talking to her would be too hard.

"So, Stacey, do you think you are responsible for your parents' happiness?" asked Kathy, the counselor sitting across from me in her office on the Sheridan campus. She was young and had a casual way about her, which relaxed me. The rising stress of working on my film had poked holes through my numbness shell. I needed to talk to a professional who didn't know me, and this time I didn't care if they were a Christian.

I looked around the room and realized that Kathy's question was a hard one for me to answer. I took a deep breath. "No, I don't think so. But I definitely try to do my best to make them happy. I don't think they could handle *two* gay kids. I know they think it's wrong, and I always try to do the right thing."

"Do *you* think it's wrong?" She asked that question so easily.

I paused. "I don't know, I'm still working on that. I have spent twelve years now trying to answer that question. I broke up with someone recently because I couldn't ask myself that anymore."

"Well, I just want to remind you it's not up to you to make your parents happy. You have to figure out what's right for *you*. It's not about them." She was good at making it feel like we were just friends talking. "As for the relationship you ended recently, were there big reasons why it wasn't working? Were you not well matched? Did you not love each other?"

I was struck at how matter-of-fact these questions were without God and faith in the equation. Not that I wanted to exclude God, but it helped me see things from a new angle.

"No, we love each other. We supported each other; we were well matched. I was just tired of the battle inside myself. I don't know if I will ever believe that being gay is okay." I was so tired of even talking about this cycle.

"Sometimes it's good to remember that life is short. It's easy to let fear rule our life if we let it. Make sure you aren't letting go of something just out of fear."

That's really good advice. I was really going to have to think about that.

I can never get this stupid sheet to fit.

As I stretched the fitted sheet across my mattress, the opposite side popped off. This shouldn't have infuriated me so much, but rage burned in my chest. I went to fix the other side, and again it popped off a corner. *That's it.* I ripped the sheet off in anger and threw it across the room.

Frustration had been building in my body for so long, and I needed a release. I pounded my firsts onto the mattress. I pounded until I couldn't pound anymore. Then I turned and flopped down on the bare mattress, exhaling loudly. This happened a lot. When things got really hard, I avoided feeling them and they came out in random moments, like trying to make the bed.

I was so *tired*. I was so *angry*. I was so *done*. I wanted to move forward in some direction, and I was so mad at myself for hurting Tams.

I decided to call her.

I dialed her number and took a deep breath.

"Hey," she answered, having seen my name on her phone. She sounded distant.

"Hey, Tams. I'm sorry. I'm just so frustrated right now, I wanted to call you."

A beat of silence. "Well, what do you want me to do about it? We haven't talked in, like, two and a half months."

She's still really hurt. Can I blame her?

"Yeah. Sorry," I said quietly.

I shouldn't have called. Now I felt worse.

"Look, Stace, I'm sorry you're frustrated, but I'm not the one to help you now." Tams sounded exhausted.

She was right. We weren't together, and I had really hurt her. This back and forth with us wasn't fair to her after all these years. She deserves more. *I can't keep doing this to her.* I couldn't turn to her for comfort now. *Damn, this sucks.*

"I'm sorry. I hope you're doing okay. I'll talk to you later," I said.

After she hung up, I sat there, noticing that the anger in my body had evaporated. I just felt deeply sad. I missed her. I missed *us*.

Kathy's words floated up in my mind like an air bubble. *Make sure you aren't letting go of something just out of fear.*

Am I letting fear rule my life?

I sat there for a moment and thought about how I felt so much frustration at myself. I screwed this up, us up, big time. And for what? Life is *so* short. How could I let this go? After these couple months on my own, I realized how much I profoundly missed her. Could we get back together? Would she let me in again?

If Tams and I were going to have another shot, I needed to talk to her in person. I was heading home for Christmas break in a couple weeks, maybe we could talk then.

I decided to do something bold, to hopefully open the door for this conversation when I went to visit. I ordered Tams's favorite flowers: two dozen pink, white, and red roses to be delivered to her. On the enclosed note, I wrote:

Tams, I'm so sorry. I don't know the future, but I know you feel like home to me.

Winter 2009

Winnipeg, Manitoba

As I walked up the steps of Tams's little house, my heart pounded. I had no idea how this would go.

I knocked on her front door and blew warm air into my hands. It was a frigid winter evening, and Christmas lights twinkled on the houses around me. Christmas had always been my favorite time of year, but right now, I couldn't care less about the season. I was hoping that if I explained how sorry I was, then maybe Tams and I could have another chance to be together.

She opened her door, a little smile forming on her lips. It was the same familiar smile I had known for so long, but it was tinged with sadness. I was glad she had at least agreed to talk with me.

"Hey." I smiled and gave a small wave.

"Hey, Stace, come in." Tams pulled the door open wider for me, and the warmth of her house welcomed me.

As we settled in her living room with fresh cups of coffee, I immediately felt comfort wrap around my nervousness.

I took a deep breath and dove in.

"So, you liked your flowers?" I gestured towards a bouquet of flowers on a nearby table.

She blushed slightly as she looked over at them. "Yeah, I did. Thank you."

"Tams, I'm so sorry for hurting you. I made some really bad choices because I felt totally overwhelmed and I shut down. Can you forgive me?" I pulled at the hem of my sweater to try to find my courage. "I still don't know if I can be gay and Christian. But I know I love you. I am wondering if you are willing to give us another chance."

I looked into her eyes and waited. It wasn't long before her dimples gave her away.

She took a deep breath. "Yes. Stace, I forgive you. You know I love you. But are you sure about this?"

"All I know is I want to move forward with you, and I am trusting the rest to work itself out. It's not going to be easy, but I don't see my life without you," I said.

She smiled. "Okay, then, let's do it."

I set down my coffee, stood up, and walked the few steps over to Tams. Taking her hands, I pulled her into a big hug that filled my body with relief When we kissed, the spinning in my chest broke through the shell of numbness.

The battle inside still tugged on my heart for attention. My struggle was not over yet. I let Tams's love wash over me, but fought to fully embrace it.

Jesus, am I truly gay? I want to make peace with myself and with you. I don't want these questions to haunt me forever. I want to be at peace with who I am, and not feel guilt or sadness. Jesus, I want kids. I want a marriage. Can I have that with Tams? Can I truly have that with her? Is this what you want for me?

I held my breath as the familiar music began, and my beloved bug, Bentley, filled the screen in the large auditorium.

For the past eight months I had worked so incredibly hard on the special two minutes of film now unfolding before our senior class. We were holding a screening of all the fourth-year films, and I was so proud of what all my classmates had created. The talent that surrounded me in this room was astounding.

Anna was sitting beside me and tapped me excitedly on the shoulder. "Ohhhh, there it is, Stace! Turned out soooo great!" She leaned in front of me to address Tams, who was on my other side. "Tams, don't you agree?"

Tams had come back to Ontario with me after Christmas break and walked the home stretch of this Sheridan road beside me. She had even helped color some of my frames of animation in the last few scrambling days.

I couldn't help but smile widely at the finished product. *My film,* Tah-Dah! It wasn't perfect, but I had done it. I had finished. I was proud of completing something so enormous.

"Thanks, Anna. Yours is coming up soon!" I said.

Tams squeezed my knee quickly and leaned in to whisper, "So great, babe. It's finished. So proud of you!"

Throughout the last few months, Tams and I had gently massaged the delicate parts of our relationship and nursed them back to life. I knew this had only been possible because our relationship had been built on such a solid foundation of friendship in the first place.

And yet . . .

Now that my Sheridan journey was coming to a close, the anarchy inside of me threatened to burst out again. I knew I loved Tams and was committed to her, that part felt settled and sure. But what about my faith? How did God actually fit in? I had been asking God to change me for years now. I never dared to ask him to bless my sexuality because I never believed he would. I was terrified of what would happen if I asked him to bless something that everyone said was so sinful . . . Every pastor I emailed, every book or article I found on homosexuality and Christianity . . . they all said the same thing in the end. "God loves you BUT . . . you are an abomination for loving a woman. Sorry, it says so in the Bible. You have to choose one." The Bible verses I had memorized since childhood felt like a trap. My faith in Jesus should be setting me free, shouldn't it? Not weighing me down and preventing me from truly living.

It was time to go there. I needed to address this final question once and for all:

Can I be both gay and Christian?

_____

Jesus, I feel lost—truly lost. I need you to intervene. Only you know the true depths of my heart, the questions I continually ask myself about my sexuality, my future. Why is it so foggy to my mind and heart? Why can't I see clearly? Jesus, bring me to a place where I can see your truth and purpose for me.

Chapter 24

Fall 2009

Winnipeg, Manitoba

I stared up at my favorite tree in Assiniboine Park, journal on my lap, noticing that the leaves looked the same as they did when I started coming here at the age of sixteen. *How is it possible that I'm twenty-nine now?* I wiped tears from my cheeks. The pandemonium in my soul had reached epic proportions. I was finding it hard to breathe or swallow properly anymore, the chaos was constricting everything.

I was back in Winnipeg after graduating from Sheridan and embarking on a couple adventures. *Tah-Dah* had gotten accepted into quite a few film festivals. Cody and I had gone to L.A. together to attend one, agreeing that he would have walked better in my heels on the red carpet than I did. Once seated in the theater, I had to catch my breath when I realized we were sitting

in front of Lena Headey. I had had a massive crush on her since seeing the lesbian movie *Imagine Me & You*.

Tams and I had also gone on an epic road trip through the States to celebrate my graduation. We drove down to San Diego, and then up the Pacific Coast Highway to Seattle and back to Winnipeg. We called it our "Bucket List Trip," stopping whenever we wanted to explore. We went on a hot-air balloon ride, we swam with dolphins, she got a tattoo. It was incredible, but I wished I felt as free as the open road before us.

Time's up. I had to deal with this. I could no longer live this way.

If I didn't do something drastic, I would truly not *want* to live this way.

A friend had recently asked me to housesit her place for a week, so here was my chance. It was time for God and me to have a nice, long, excruciating talk.

Just me and God.

<hr>

"I'm sorry, babe. I have to do this. I think we both know this has been coming for a very long time."

I sat on the edge of Tams's bed. This bed, where we had discovered every beautifully intimate detail about each other over these seven tumultuous years. Tender, soft, breathless memories flitted in front of my eyes, jump-

starting the familiar spinning sensation. Would this be the last time I would sit here as her girlfriend?

She sat across from me, head in her hands, tears escaping between her fingers.

"I know. I know you do. It's just been such a long road."

I walked around the bed and over to her, gently took her hands, and wrapped mine around them. I collapsed against her soft, warm chest and began to cry under the weight of what was in front of me. I didn't want to leave this person who felt like home to me, the strong arms wrapped around me.

Why can't I just let myself fully embrace it?

"I wish I didn't have to spend this time alone. I wish I didn't have to make this decision. But I can't live with this turmoil inside anymore—I just can't. And I can't keep dragging you along. If I can't be gay and Christian, it's not fair to you. If I truly decide that, I need to let you go. I need this time alone with God to figure it out for good. It's time."

"I just . . . love you. I don't want to lose you." Tams closed her eyes tight, releasing fresh streams of tears.

Slowly, I pulled her lips to mine, tasting their heartbreaking saltiness. In that moment of familiar intimacy, I wondered, would this be the last time we kissed? I had to prepare myself for that possibility, because I truly did not know what my time alone this week would bring.

God, help me find the right path, right path, right path . . .

Father, please go before me on this week spending time alone. I am scared. I want to hear your voice. I want to make a decision and move forward, knowing it is the right one. Whatever that means.

My friend's house was in the opposite corner of the city from my parents' place, which was helpful. Since Cody's wedding last year, my parents had been distant, angry, and sad. It was so hard for me to be near them.

I dropped my overnight bags onto the guest bed in the basement and let out a huge sigh of emotional exhaustion. My friend's house was big and empty, and I welcomed the silence. It felt comforting in contrast to all the noise crowding my mind and heart.

This was the perfect opportunity to reflect on my life. In the past, I had experienced many pivotal moments during weeks set aside specifically to connect with God. My week at summer camp each year while I was growing up always left me with greater clarity and a renewed feeling of connection to God. I thought back now to that critical week at camp when I was sixteen and fell in love with Joanna. That had marked the beginning of my long struggle of wrestling with my attraction to girls.

Then I thought about my week in California with Kassidy. I had gone to the Exodus conference expecting God to "fix" me, but instead I discovered it was impossible for me to be ex-gay.

Now I had been dating Tams for seven years. I felt God speaking to my spirit. I was ready for something big to happen. I knew that by the end of the week, somehow I had to make a decision and finally move forward.

My choices were:

Embrace and celebrate being gay and Christian, and move forward with Tams.

OR

Realize I can never reconcile my Christianity AND my gayness, let Tams go, and try my best to live a Christian life.

I retrieved my journal from my bag and collapsed onto the bed. I needed to get out the thoughts as they came.

God, I know you have provided this time for me to be alone with you. Empty me, I pray. May this be a serious step toward you and toward having clarity in this chaos. Is my fear of losing Tams preventing me from doing what I need to do? Do I truly feel it is wrong to be gay? Or maybe, am I scared of admitting to the Christian world that I am gay? I have so much doubt about what is right and what is wrong, what is real love or not. Oh, please speak to me. I'm so lost.

The anxiety constricted my throat. I needed to move the energy through my body. Time to go to the kitchen and make some tea and settle in for this weeklong journey. As I made my way up the stairs, I knew one thing.

The Bible told me that God wanted me to have life, and to have it *abundantly*.

Okay, Stace, it's time to fight tooth and nail for my abundance.

———

It was a beautiful early fall evening, the crickets were beginning to sing, and the air was thick with the warmth left over from the hot prairie summer.

Sitting on the back deck at my friend's house, I looked up from my writing and stared into the large empty field that backed onto her property. It was comforting to see so much open space. Maybe if I stared long enough, I would find the answers I was looking for.

It was the middle of my week alone, and I was exhausted in every way. And so, *so* lonely. When I'm hurting, I'm terrible at being alone. But I was

committed to shutting myself into my friend's house—no phone calls or emails to the outside world.

But, *damn*, it was hard.

This sacred space, where I had invited only God in—this was our time to have it out. The gloves were off, and I made sure to throw every hurtful, terrible, embarrassing, shameful, impossible question at him. I needed to get it out. *All* of it. Every moment I'd struggled with this, every tear I'd cried for the last thirteen years—they had all led to this week.

I relived it all. The shame and turmoil of my relationship with Joanna. The crippling heartbreak of missing my chance with Megyn. The confusion over dating Justin, and the guilt of disappointing my parents. The pull of infatuation with Kassidy. The deep love and intense ups and downs of my relationship with Tams.

Throughout the week I had journaled, prayed, paced, cried, dreamed, accused, grieved. Now I took a deep breath and continued to write out my questions.

I can't do this alone. But I can do all things through Christ, who strengthens me. Can you show me that is real, Jesus? Can we do this? I am scared. I cling to you in this storm. I feel empty and weak tonight. I need you to fill me. I don't know if I can see through this to make a decision. Please fill this space in my heart . . . in my pain.

I woke up to the bright morning sunlight seeping in through the closed blinds.

As I blinked myself awake, I remembered that this was my last day here. Fear flooded my stomach. *Will I really leave here with a decision and feel peace?*

I got up, showered, and made some coffee. Grabbing my journal, I headed to the back deck, where the fresh air could ease my rising anxiety. I settled into the chair, closed my eyes, and allowed myself to enjoy the warmth of the sun on my face.

I felt God whisper to me, *I am here. Just ask me.*

I opened my eyes and began to write.

What have you planned for my life, God? How can I fulfill that purpose? Is Tams just my best friend or is she the one you have made for me? Would you bless our home? Our relationship? If we got married? If we had kids? I feel at peace with her, I feel like myself, safe and loved. Could you possibly be asking me to be an example of someone who is totally committed to you, yet loves another woman? Am I scared to believe that?

I felt God slowly helping me paint the full picture of our relationship. I wrote it down in black and white—what I knew for certain:

Tams loves me in spite, and because, of my flaws.
She pushes me to pursue truth, honesty, and my dreams.
She allows space for me to be the best version of myself.
She loves gently and with no conditions.
She is love waiting for me.

I paused and reread that list. I read it again, and then again. It struck me.
This is how it feels to be perfectly loved.
Isn't this how you say you love us, God?
Was it possible that through my relationship with Tams, I had come to understand God more? Was there—could there possibly be—a way to have *both* the relationship with God, *and* the relationship with Tams?
Wait.
For so many years, I had been asking myself and other Christians if I could be gay *and* Christian. But did I ever honestly turn my face toward heaven and ask *God*? I had never had the courage to do that.
Until today.
I closed my eyes, took a deep breath, and prayed:

Please, God . . . Jesus . . . I want to yell and say that I am gay. I want to lay it all down, and I want you to bless my life. I love Tams. Can I take her hand, and ask you to be in the middle?

I held my breath and listened.

*

*

*

*

A tingling started on the top of my head.

A warm sensation slowly began to wash over me.

Softly—like the sun gently kissing my skin on the first day of summer—it began to travel down my body.

I heard a still small voice reply to my innermost being:

Yes.

Yes!

A resounding yes!

In that moment, a soft peace rained down on me. Gently at first. Then it gave way to a torrential downpour. I felt it washing away the years of chaos that had lived there for so long.

Peace.

Full, soft, healing . . . *peace.* In that moment, I finally allowed this truth to enter my heart and resonate deep within. The fears in my head and fears of what God's people thought of me were no match for the perfect love of God himself.

God said to me: *I made you, ALL of you. Fearfully and wonderfully.*

I covered my face with my hands and cried in sweet and long-deserved relief.

This is who I am. And it is good.

The cracks and scars from my journey would be the sacred spaces where I let the light in. Somehow, I knew, nothing I had experienced would be discounted or wasted.

I couldn't wait to collapse into Tams's arms, for good.

Jesus, today I am taking a leap of faith. This peace you have given me is like nothing I have felt in thirteen years. I want to commit first to you and second to Tams. I lay it all down at your feet and ask you to bless us, our relationship, our future together. I love you, God. Keep opening my eyes every day. I let go of this fear and doubt for good and leave it in your hands!

I knocked on Tams's front door, vibrating with pure joy. Peace flowed through me, coating every space like a soothing balm. A Bible verse I had learned long ago at camp popped into my mind:

If God is for us, then who can be against us?

Tams hadn't heard from me since I had left for my week alone, but it felt like a few months had passed. She opened the door, eyes tired and red. I heard her catch her breath when she saw me.

I wasted no time.

"Yes. We—you, me, and God—we can do this. Together."

The look that came over her face when I said those words—that's what freedom looks like.

And as I kissed her lips in a flurried celebratory embrace, I thought, *This is what freedom* feels *like.*

Chapter 25

Spring 2010

Winnipeg, Manitoba

I heard Tams's voice beside me. "Okay, open."

I opened my eyes to discover a little square box perched atop the pillow on my lap. It took me a second. *What am I looking at?* But then it all made sense, why she had been acting so nervous earlier that evening.

It's a ring box.

"Well . . . open it." Her blue eyes sparkled with joy as she smiled and sat up straighter in the bed beside me.

As if in slow motion, I eased open the black velvet box. Inside, a beautiful brushed-silver band shone up at me.

"I had it made." She couldn't contain the details any longer. "I designed it as three simple bands, put together. The thinner, outside bands represent

223

you and me. The thicker, middle band represents God, always keeping us together."

How ironic. So many Christians would believe this was the most sinful relationship, and yet, it was, literally, God centered.

"It's just so . . . perfect." I stared at the ring's precious details, turning it over between my fingers.

"So . . . is that a yes?" Tams's gaze invited my love forever. "Stace . . . will you marry me?"

The rush of love that filled my heart in that moment was overwhelming. *What did I do to deserve this?*

"Yes! Oh man, yes. I will absolutely marry you!" I grabbed her face and let myself enjoy kissing her with no strings of shame attached. It was such a wonderful sensation.

Until a few months ago, this marriage proposal would have sent me onto an endless seesaw of doubt. But not now. Not with this peace inside that echoed so loud and true. Now I smiled at the thought of getting gay-married.

All I had ever wanted was a life of authenticity. Tams knew and respected that, and had waited to propose until she knew I finally felt okay about our life together. What a gift to be able to relax into this sea of peace and enjoy the healing effect of its waves.

Father, today Tams and I got engaged! I can't believe it either. I trust you are doing good work within me, and that you have our future in your hands. May Tams and I be an example of love to the world that we can love you and also each other. We can break the mold—with your help. Please bless what is before us: jobs, love, marriage, babies. Please walk with us down each of these roads.

Waking up cuddled next to Tams's soft, warm body, I knew this was where I was meant to be. I no longer awoke to waves of guilt, but to contentment. My chest spun as I remembered our most intimate moments from the previous night. Sex after finding peace is definitely much more enjoyable than sex riddled with shame and doubt.

As I lay in the stillness, the morning after getting engaged, I pulled my arms out from under the covers and stared incredulously at my engagement band. I touched it gingerly, still not used to seeing it there. I smiled. I knew this meant something life changing. I was choosing this life with Tams. I was choosing to marry her. I was choosing public authenticity as a gay Christian.

It was time to be open and honest with everyone in my life and to come out of the closet of shame once and for all. I desperately wanted to rip off the band-aid and shout from the rooftops that I finally had peace about who God made me to be.

But I knew that before I could tell anyone else, I needed to tell my parents. One last time.

I closed my eyes in dread.

"Are you sure you don't want me to come in with you?" Tams asked as we sat in the car outside my parents' house.

Fear and anxiety sloshed around my insides. I was at peace with our engagement, but terrified to tell them about it. I knew they would not approve or understand, even remotely.

I took a deep breath. "No. I need to do this alone."

She took my hand and placed it between hers. The warmth was comforting.

"I love you. You can do this." Her courage was always steady. I tried to soak it up.

"Love you, too. I'll be back." I smiled wearily, got out of the car, and walked toward the hardest conversation of my life.

"Hey, Stace! What a nice surprise!" My mom was in the kitchen stirring something on the stove when I entered. It was Sunday afternoon, so I had figured they would both be home.

"Hey. Um, I was wondering, can I talk to you and Dad?" My voice wavered.

I saw the familiar twinge in my mom's face. *Please, no, not again*, it said.

"Okaaaayy . . . yeah. I think Dad is in the bedroom. We can go in there."

God, please help me do this. I know it will be excruciating, but I need them to hear it from me. Please . . . help me.

I followed her down the hallway, past my childhood bedroom where so many years ago I first hid and wrote about my struggle. I felt in my bones that this would be a turning point, both for me and for my parents. My entire body tensed as I walked into battle.

"Hey, hon," my mom said to my dad, who was sitting on their bed watching TV. "Stace wants to talk to us."

My dad looked up and smiled as I entered the room. "Hey, Stace!" He turned off the TV, and my mom joined him on their bed. I sat on the floor nearby.

"Hey, there's leftover Gondola pizza in the fridge," Dad said as he settled in to listen. It was our favorite. I felt terrible.

I tried to sound normal. "Thanks, maybe later."

I looked down and spied my engagement ring. A wave of sheer panic shot through me. *Have they noticed it yet?* I cleared my throat and pushed the words out of my mouth.

"So, something happened, and I wanted you to hear it from me first. Tams and I got engaged. We are going to get married." I felt myself shifting into numb protection mode.

My mom's body stiffened, and her face clouded with anger. My dad exhaled in disappointment and looked away.

"No, that's not possible," Mom spat.

"I'm sorry . . ." I stammered. "I'm sorry . . . but it is." I hated seeing how upset they both were. I was breaking their hearts. I was failing them.

They had gone through this with Cody a couple years ago and were still weary from that battle. Now it was happening all over again with me, the "good" one.

My mom narrowed her eyes at me. "You can't give in to this. You can't. If you give in to this, God will never be able to use you for good. And more than that, anything that you have done for him up to this point will be null and void."

Ouch, that hurts. God, is that true? I felt myself crack under the pressure.

I dug deeper for courage. "I don't believe that. I have peace about this. I just wanted to be honest and tell you guys first."

I couldn't hold their gaze anymore. I looked down at the soft blue carpet. I felt like I was turning inside out with discomfort. I wanted to run out of there.

My mom's tone kicked up a notch to exasperated fury. "No. No, I don't believe that. Absolutely not!"

Finally, my dad spoke. He sounded frustrated—a tone he rarely used with me. "I thought you were over this." His clear disappointment cut deep.

"No. I mean, I tried . . . for *so* many years, I tried. But now I believe this is who I am."

Then he tried using logic. "Look, it's unfortunate, but everyone has something they struggle with, right? It's like alcoholism. This is yours. But it doesn't mean you can just give in to it."

My head was swimming and my heart was sinking. I didn't know how to respond. I grabbed at one last desperate surge of fearlessness. *Get it all out now.*

"I don't believe that. I don't struggle with it anymore. God gave me peace, and Tams and I are going to have a life together," I said.

This was the final nail in the coffin for my mom. She got up and started to pace the room.

"No! No, you will *not*! This will *not* happen!" The combination of outrage and disgust scared me.

I tried desperately to hold back the sobs climbing up my throat.

"I'm sorry! I'm so sorry, but this *is* going to happen!" I started to panic.

My dad was outright angry now too. "Listen. If you asked one hundred pastors what they thought about homosexuality, and most of them said it was wrong, you would *have* to agree it's wrong, right?" He threw the question at me like a fireball.

I couldn't think properly. "No. It doesn't work that way."

He pressed further. His anger was unsettling as he repeated his point more forcefully: "You have to agree with that, right? And guaranteed, most pastors would agree that it's wrong!"

A sob escaped my throat. I could barely speak, but I managed, "No, I can't agree. I'm sorry." I wiped away the tears sliding down my cheeks. I couldn't let them see my weakness.

My dad let out a frustrated sigh. "Well, you just aren't thinking right. You *have* to agree with that."

I sat there on the floor, trying to stifle my despair. I felt unsafe.

My mom crossed her arms and stated with finality, "We will never be happy about this. We will never celebrate this. *God* will never celebrate this."

I had to get out of there. I could barely breathe. I had done what I came to do, but I felt like my heart was collapsing in on itself. I got up and wiped more tears from my cheeks.

"I'm sorry. I'm so sorry you don't want me to be this way, but this is who I am. I love you both, and I'm sorry for disappointing you. Tams and I are getting married. I'm going to go now before this gets worse."

I forced myself to turn and leave their bedroom. I held my breath and held in most of the pain all the way down the hallway, through the kitchen, and out the front door—until I got back to Tams.

I collapsed into the passenger seat and burst into sobs. I had never felt such visceral grief before. I had never gone against my parents' wishes to such a degree. I had crushed their dreams for me, and there was no going back.

But I had no choice. *This is who I am.* I had to be honest about it, especially to them.

Tams sat quietly. She knew no words would soothe my pain. She reached over and wrapped her arm around me, holding me tightly as I released sobs of despair and tears of heartache. Deep inside, I felt God gently reminding me that he had given me this peace for a reason. I just needed to rest in it.

We backed out of the driveway and headed toward Tams's house. The hardest part was over.

———

God, this has been so hard. I hate hurting my parents. But I was thinking . . . I have always felt that you have a big plan for me. That my life will mean something. Is it to stand up for you as I love Tams? To show the world that this is okay? I seek you today.

Chapter 26

Summer 2010

Winnipeg, Manitoba

God, deep down I feel blessed. Being in the position of "gay Christian" won't be easy, but it will open up so many opportunities for me to share your love and grace, on both "sides." Please use me. I feel I need to share what you have done in my life. Please give me a heart for others in both the Christian and LGBT communities. Show me how to love those like my parents and my friends who don't understand.

I was *so* nervous.

Before the news spread like wildfire, I wanted to tell a few close friends in person about who I was, and about Tams and me getting engaged. Tonight I was meeting Rebecca at a coffee shop, and I had no idea how it was going to go.

This conversation was going to be tough. Rebecca had a history with both Tams and me, having been Tams's roommate. Rebecca and I naturally made everything silly and light. Even now, sitting opposite each other, we laughed over something ridiculous. *How do I switch gears and just come out?* As I waited for the right moment, I realized this was something straight people never had to think about. They were already "out."

"Oh boy, that's hilarious!" I said, then shifted to a more serious tone. I had to take the plunge. "Anyway, I do want to talk to you about something else."

She wiped tears from her eyes from laughing so hard. "Sure, of course."

"Okay, I'm just going to say it. I'm gay. And, well, Tams and I have been dating for a really long time, and we just got engaged. I'm sorry we've been keeping it from you. It took me so long to be okay with myself."

I saw in Rebecca's expression that I had blindsided her.

"Uh—what?" she stammered.

Oh, no. This was definitely not going well.

I braced myself and kept going. "Yeah. I know it's a lot. I'm still a Christian, though. God has given me peace about it." I wished I could explain this feeling that swam freely inside of me, but no

236

words could do it justice. Rebecca looked at the floor, apparently searching for something to say.

She looked at me, all the joy from a minute ago gone. "Stace, how can you and Tams embrace this lifestyle? How can you give in to this sin and walk away from God?"

God, help me do this.

"Rebecca, I wish I could explain this to you. I know it looks like I am walking away from God, but actually, I'm running toward him. I know this is who he made me to be, and now I'm just being honest about it," I said gently.

Her body tensed. She sat back in her chair. "But . . . you're gay. You can't be a Christian *and* be gay." She looked away. I could tell she felt betrayed. "Stace, you *can't*. The Bible says it's wrong. And how could you lie to me all this time?"

This is why it had been impossible to be honest. I knew people would respond like this. This is so unfair.

I could feel our friendship slipping through my fingers, simply because I wanted to be authentic.

I kept trying. "Rebecca, I know it's hard to believe and that it's not what we have been taught. I never intended to lie to you. But please listen when I say, I have pursued God for *thirteen years*, and he is the one who gave me this freedom. I'm still a Christian. And yes, I'm gay. But I'm still Stace."

This was too much for her to process. I could feel it. All she saw now were those three letters: *g-a-y.*

Rebecca looked out the coffee shop window and sighed. "I just can't support this. I'm sorry, I wish I could, but it's my duty as a Christian to remind you that this is sin. I know you don't want to believe it, but this is so wrong."

In that moment, our friendship fell apart in front of me.

———

"You and Tams are *engaged*?!" Ashley shrieked.

I laughed with relief at her response to my big news. My conversation with Rebecca, then later with Lisa and other friends from church, had certainly not gone this well. Thankfully, when I finally got up the nerve to call

Anna, she had been gracious and excited for me and Tams. She and I were still close from our years together at Sheridan, and since she knew Tams too, I had asked her to be a bridesmaid. I was grateful I wouldn't be losing my friendship with my "little sister."

Now I was so happy that Ashley and I had chosen to get together at our favorite pizza place, because from now on, I would remember this great moment every time I came back.

"Yes! I'm sorry I didn't tell you earlier. It's been such a long journey." I relaxed and took a big bite of my pizza. I had hoped Ashley would see the real me, especially after knowing me most of my life.

"Oh heavens, who cares about that! Tell me about the wedding!" she exclaimed. "Have you guys started planning yet? Have you started dress shopping?"

Suddenly sadness mixed with my excitement. I had never thought about going wedding-dress shopping without my mom.

I tried to shake off the grief. "No, not yet, but soon. Anyway, I wanted to ask—will you be one of our bridesmaids?"

Ashley swallowed and nodded furiously. "*Will* I? Can we cheers, please?"

We tapped our large plastic cups of iced tea together, and as I took a swallow, I tasted real joy.

———

The hot sun shone down on us in Tams's aunt's backyard, where her extended family had gathered for our engagement barbecue. We were playing bocce ball with her cousins, and the air was full of laughter.

Tams's grandma was enjoying watching us play. "You almost got that, there, Stace!" As I came near, she smiled. Then she reached for my hand and pulled me in for a tight hug. I absorbed some of that special sort of healing love that comes from grandmothers.

Tams's mom smiled and I moved over to give her a side hug. Tams overcame her own challenges in her journey with her family, but I was so grateful for this day when we could all celebrate. I felt ten times lighter now that my whole world knew the real me, and the truth about us. I allowed myself to marinate in the acceptance offered by Tams's family. It was so healing. But it was also hard to understand, because of how difficult it had been with my family.

These last couple months had been filled with ups and downs as I shared the news with family and friends. Some opened their arms; others walked away. Once we put it out on Facebook that we were engaged, I braced myself for the gossip to spread fast, and it did. I got many hurtful private messages from well-meaning Christians. Having Tams's family embrace us was huge. At the same time, I found it a bit troubling because I knew it was largely because they weren't Christians.

I heard cheers and looked over as Tams threw her bocce ball closest to the center, winning for her team. As I watched her, my heart swelled. She laughed easily. I could feel her contentment, even from across the lawn. The love we shared was so grounding.

In a few months, she will be my wife.

I couldn't wait.

Chapter 27

Winnipeg, Manitoba

"Stace, come out," called Cody from outside my changing room. "We want to see!"

I was looking at myself in the mirror, standing in a fancy white wedding dress, and it felt . . . wrong. I looked so strange, reflected back at myself. *I better go show them anyway.*

Carefully, I walked out to the large wall of mirrors and stepped up onto the carpeted riser. Cody, Eric, and Tams had all come with me to dress-shop. Tams already knew she didn't want a conventional wedding dress, but I wasn't sure.

I was marrying a woman, so nothing would be traditional. I needed to figure out each step as I went. When I allowed myself to let go of the fear, it was quite freeing to be able to choose what fit *me*, and not what was expected.

I saw Tams's dimpled smile in the mirror behind me. "Stace, you look beautiful. But . . . you don't look comfortable." She knew me well.

"Uh, yeah, you look awkward." Cody was always honest.

It made me laugh. "I know, right? This is so not me!"

The shop owner came over. "Oh, let me try one more thing! Here's this veil . . ." She nestled it in the back of my hair and fluffed it out down my back.

Okay, now I know *this is definitely not me.* Cody, Eric, and Tams must have seen my expression because they all started laughing. I couldn't help but join in.

"Thank you, but I don't think this is for me." I said, making every attempt to be polite and to stifle my laughter.

As I changed back into my regular clothes, I was struck by these unexpected moments of joy. My mom wasn't with me, and I didn't want a traditional wedding dress. But I was with people who love me, and I was choosing authenticity every step of the way.

That felt *so* good.

I spoke into the quiet morning stillness. "Babe, what do you think? I'm feeling overwhelmed."

Tams and I were lying in bed on a Saturday morning, slipping in and out of sleep. The birds chirped outside her window. It was peaceful in a sense, but my thoughts were all over the place.

Tams rolled over to face me and spoke groggily. "What, babe? You have to fill me in here."

"We are both Christians. We love each other and God—and yet we aren't allowed to get married in Soul Sanctuary or Calvary Temple. Pastor Gabe would never marry us." I sighed heavily. "I just have moments when that sinks in, and I feel sad."

Tams snuck her arm under the blankets and around my middle and pulled me to her. My body instantly relaxed at her warm touch.

"Hey, listen. Didn't we agree that the space at the hotel is going to be amazing? That long white sunlit hallway is just right for our ceremony, and everyone can enjoy breakfast right afterward at the reception. Also, mimosas." She leaned over and kissed my cheek. "We couldn't have mimosas at church, right?"

I smiled. She was right. "But we're getting married on a Sunday morning. Do you think people will assume we are doing that purposely to anger Christians? A gay wedding to replace church?" My mind did a lot of spiral thinking if I let it.

"Babe! God will be there. We will be there. People who love us will be there. And, cinnamon buns." She smiled. Somehow she always managed to slow my spinning thoughts. "It will be perfect."

I rolled over and gave her a kiss. "You're right. I love you."

Tams lay her head on my arm. "We better get up and get ready if we're going to meet with that officiant today. Hopefully she'll be a great fit for our breakfast-mimosa-non-church-but-also-God wedding."

"Brat!" I snuck my hand behind her knee to tickle her, and we both giggled.

"Babe, I've been thinking," Tams said, taking a bite of her hash browns.

We were back at Stella's, the place where we had built our friendship. We had revisited this cozy restaurant frequently throughout our relationship, and were now finishing up our wedding-planning here.

"You've been applying for animation jobs for a while, but there are no jobs in Winnipeg, right? I mean, we'll have to move eventually, right?"

I was intrigued. "Yeah, right. We'll have to move eventually when I get a job."

"Well, what if we just decided to move to where the jobs are, and then you apply? Why don't we just take a risk? What do we have to lose?" Tams smiled.

247

Excitement started to build in my chest. "Hmm . . . we *could* . . . why not? But where? If we move without jobs, we would probably have to stay in Canada because it's so impossible to get visas for working in the States. Plus the healthcare is so bad there and gay marriage isn't even legal."

"What about Vancouver? We already spent a lot of time near Toronto when you went to Sheridan. People retire to the mountains. Why don't we try to make a life there?" Tams's eyes sparkled.

Something about this suggestion lit a fire inside me. It felt right.

I couldn't stop myself from breaking into a smile. "Oh my word, yes! What if we did that? *Could* we do that?"

"Why not? We can always move back to Winnipeg if it doesn't work out," Tams encouraged.

"Okay. Yes, let's do it!" We clinked our coffee mugs.

Jesus, I feel in my heart that this life is too short. I want to step out in faith! I want to wake up every morning, next to the person I love and be surrounded by your natural beauty. Please clear the path for us to move to Vancouver. Please give us the words to say to Mom and Dad. Prepare their hearts, please.

I was so incredibly uncomfortable.

Each time these conversations happened, I could tolerate less. I was glad Tams and I had decided to do this one together.

We were sitting in my parents' basement on the L-shaped couch, Tams and I, across from Mom and Dad. I knew it was difficult for Tams to be there, knowing my parents' absolute disapproval of our engagement. But I admired this facet of her love that was courageous and protective of what we had.

My mom couldn't hold back her feelings. "Are you serious? You two are going to move across the country together? That's not only foolish, but because of your choice to have a *union*, God will not bless your life together."

I tried to stay calm so we could get through this. "Mom, it's not a union. We are getting *married*. We are going to have a *wedding*."

She crossed her arms. "Nope. A wedding and a marriage are sanctioned by God only to be between a man and a woman. This is a *union*. And frankly, it's not right."

Her barrage of judgmental declarations overwhelmed me. My chest tightened.

"I'm sorry you feel that way. But we *are* getting married in the spring, and we *are* moving to Vancouver in a couple months. It's the right choice for us," I said with as much strength as I could muster.

"Stacey," my mom said angrily. She rarely called me by my full name. It vibrated in my body. "If you had a *Christian* daughter, and she wanted to move across the country and live with her *sex partner*, would you be happy?"

Wow, that's a low blow. Tams had been a faithful support in my life now for over seven years. *Why does she have to reduce everything to sex?* I didn't know how to respond. I noticed that my dad seemed uncomfortable too. I got the sense he didn't want to fight like this anymore. But she continued with intensity. "You know in your heart what is right. You know God believes that homosexuality is disgusting. I know one day you will see the light."

I could no longer suppress my anger. "Mom, this is who I am. Are you outright saying *I* am disgusting?"

She narrowed her eyes at me. Her silence was the *yes* I desperately did not want to hear.

I felt Tams's energy explode beside me. She had heard enough.

"Okay, I need to say something, so please *do not* interrupt me."

She was pissed. I did not see this side of Tams often, but I was grateful she was letting it show in this moment.

She spoke through low-level rage. "How can you be so awful to your own daughter? She is trying to be honest. She has been trying to do the right thing for the past *fourteen years*! I think that you are hypocritical and judgmental, and that the way you love Stace is conditional. Which is *not* the way that God loves us. You have no right to speak on behalf of God for Stace's life, or for our marriage. We are going to have a life together, and God *will* bless it. End of story."

My mom was shocked into silence. Tams had never spoken up to her before. My dad, incredibly, was gently nodding in agreement. I knew he was in an impossible spot, wanting to support his wife and daughter on opposite sides.

I felt such massive relief to have someone stand up for me.

I wanted to *sob* with relief.

I would never have to do this journey alone again.

Chapter 28

Spring 2011

Winnipeg, Manitoba

I clicked my pen nervously as I stared at the majestic mountains of British Columbia through the airplane window. Tams's hand reached over to gently calm me.

We had just departed from Vancouver for Winnipeg, a few days before our wedding, and I was awhirl with emotions and thoughts. It felt so strange to fly home, knowing I would not see my parents. They hadn't wanted to know when our wedding was, and I couldn't visit them and pretend it was a normal trip home. We were flying home *to get married*. I wanted to be able to celebrate and gush about it. But not seeing them at all was heartbreaking.

"Maybe you'll feel better if we go over that?" Tams gestured to our thick wedding planner in my lap.

I took a deep breath and focused on happier things. "Yes! Okay, we have to check with our florist tomorrow. Anna will be flying in from Toronto in the morning, so someone has to pick her up. And we are doing dinner with our bridesmaids, right?" I covered my eyes with my hand. "Oh, why did I say I would sing a song with my guitar in our ceremony? I wanted to do it for you, but I forgot there would be a bunch of other people there!"

Tams smiled as I rattled things off. "Babe, don't worry. It's all going to be fine. Let's just try to relax and let things unfold. In a few days, we will be married!"

I leaned over and kissed her soft lips. "I can't wait."

———

It was the day before the wedding, and Tams and I had booked separate hotel rooms, each staying with a couple of our bridesmaids.

Anna, Ashley, and I had been laughing and enjoying cheap champagne, but as they searched for the next episode of *Say Yes to the Dress*, it hit me. Some of the dreams that I had once had—*that my parents had*—were fading away in front of me.

Tomorrow would be the antithesis of what I knew as a typical Christian wedding. I would be marrying a woman and asking God to bless us. We would not be in a church. My parents and extended family would not be there. *Can I really do this?* It suddenly felt strange and scary and . . . sad. I began to cry.

Anna and Ashley tried their best to comfort me, but finally, one of them went to get Tams. She sat down gently beside me on the bed. She held my hand and spoke softly. "I know it's hard, babe. I'm sorry this isn't a time of just celebration for you. I'm sorry you're feeling such heartbreak."

I sniffled and wiped my nose with a tissue.

"Yeah. And it's not that I doubt *us*. I'm just . . . sad. Why is this so hard? I wish they could be here." Saying it out loud brought a fresh wave of tears.

"I know, hon. But you can't control the way they think, the way they feel. They still love you, but they just . . . can't support this. I know your dad is struggling, though."

"What do you mean?" I sniffled.

"He called me tonight," she said.

"*What?*"

"Yeah. He must have asked Cody what day our wedding was. He wanted to talk to you, but I told him that wouldn't be a good idea. He said he felt bad about everything. I know this is hard for him."

I closed my eyes and released more tears. I didn't want to go against my parents, and they didn't want me to make this choice. But here we were. My dad and I had always been close. This must be tearing him apart.

"I feel bad that he's having a hard time," I said quietly.

"I know, babe. Try to focus on the love that we have, and the people who will be here tomorrow who *want* to be here. This is *our day*, and we are going to enjoy it. I love you, my almost-wife." She squeezed my hand.

I smiled despite the tears still rolling down my cheeks. This was where I was meant to be. I exhaled grief, and inhaled joy. I lifted Tams's hand and kissed it.

"I love you too, my almost-wife."

Today's the day.

It was the morning of Sunday, May 15, 2011. I closed my eyes and breathed in the smell of fresh flowers filling the room. A white orchid was in my hair, my makeup had been done by a friend, and I wore a simple paisley dress that Tams and I had picked out together. Clutching Cody on one side and Eric on the other, I carefully made my way down the aisle toward my future wife.

My Tams.

My wedding day was not at all what I envisioned as a little girl.

But what a beautiful day it was.

Love was there.

God is here.

I breathed in this moment deeply, and with each step, I realized I only felt love. I was wrapped tightly in it like a swaddled newborn. The room was full of joy and support. There was no space left for my sadness or grief. This feeling, like the peace I had been given a year and a half ago, was a gift. I caught Tams's grandma's eye, and she gently nodded her encouragement. I noticed all our bridesmaids wiping tears away already. Each of them had come to celebrate our love through her own unique journey of affirmation. I was grateful for them all. In that moment, I didn't feel the loss of my parents' presence—only the love of God, and of the people there.

As I walked toward Tams, I felt God say to me:

"This is who I have made for you."

I smiled as I looked into her face. She smiled back and tearfully watched me make my way home to her. She looked so beautiful in her soft brown pants, blue blouse, and powder-blue cardigan, colors that matched my dress perfectly. She had even let our friend do her makeup.

Cody, Eric, and I stopped in front of Tams and the officiant, and I hugged Eric. I turned to Cody, and we did an excited double high-five, because that's more our style, and then hugged amid our guests' and our own laughter. It had been a long journey for us both. I was so glad he was here for me.

Tams extended her hand. I took it, and stood to face my future.

Tams spoke first, holding a wedding band that matched my engagement ring. Inscribed on each of the bands we would exchange was our wedding date and *Love you more*.

"Stace. I promise to always defend your right to be you—courageous, honest, full of light. I promise to be your playmate who, even at times when it seems silly or inappropriate, will dance with you as though no one is watching. I promise to encourage you in your dreams, and work hand in hand as we build new dreams together. I promise that when this life brings you sorrow, I will hold the umbrella while you hold on to me.

"Today I pledge my endless love to you. I promise to be your faithful lover, your steadfast companion, your best friend, your greatest cheerleader, and above all, to hold you gently, but firmly, as the love of my life, as long as we both shall live."

I looked into those eyes that had captivated me so many years ago and tried not to let tears stop me from saying the words I had waited so long to say.

My turn.

"Tams, throughout the last seven years of walking side by side, you have been there in my deepest valleys, quietly holding my hand. You have been there on my highest mountaintops, proudly shouting my name. No matter our opposition, no matter our trials, you were there to shower me with unimaginable grace, love, and tenderness.

"I sincerely believe that our lives are a blink of an eye, and that's why right now, today, in front

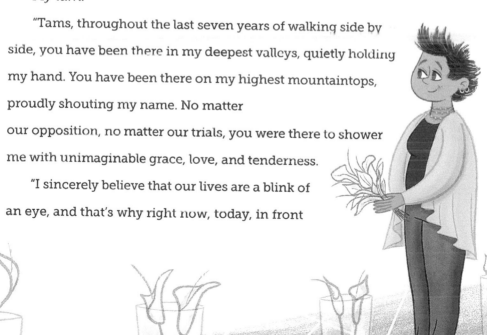

of God and our friends and family, I ecstatically ask you to be my wife. In thick, in thin, in young, in old, in life and in death.

"As someone more articulate than me once said: 'Across the years, I will walk with you in deep green forests, and shores of sand, and when our time on earth is through, in heaven too, I will hold your hand.' I promise to love you with all that I am, for now, for always, forever. Because to me, my Tams, you are perfect."

We stood facing each other, in awe of this love we shared. I smiled at the tears sparkling in her eyes.

The officiant spoke in a voice that exuded joy. "Tams, do you take Stacey as your wife, and promise to love her as long as you both shall live?"

"I do," Tams said.

I gently slid the wedding band onto her ring finger.

"Stacey, do you take Tams as your wife, and promise to love her as long as you both shall live?"

"I sure do!" I smiled widely as a couple tears escaped.

Tams carefully placed the wedding band on my finger, slid it on, and squeezed my hand.

The officiant smiled at the crowd. "With the power vested in me, I now pronounce you *wife* and *wife*!"

Tams grabbed my face and pulled it to hers as our crowd of supporters stood and cheered. This kiss was bursting at the seams with joy.

In this moment I knew: *I have found my right path.*

Today my broken and mended spirit sang.

Dear younger (gay) Stace,

People almost blew out your flame of hope, but
    you held firmly onto that little spark.

I'm so happy to tell you that today,
    that little spark is a raging wildfire!

Because you didn't give up on your fight for love,
    hope won, and authenticity reigns, both in your
heart and in your life. Today, you and Tams
have been happily married for ten wonderful years.
    That peace has never wavered. As a result of the
love you share, you now dance together in your
    living room with your 5-year-old daughter named
Robson, & your 3-year-old son named Hudson.

Don't let yourself believe
  any of the lies. One
day God will certainly
use your journey —
every _heartbreaking_
    step of it.

One day, I promise,
  it gets _so_ much
      better.

Dear Reader,

When God gave me this peace in 2010, I felt God ask something of me. In return for this gift, God asked me to share my story whenever the opportunity came up. (I never imagined it would be a book like this, though!) I have always tried to listen, because maybe someone needed to hear it. If I can help by being open and honest, then I won't hesitate. I believe we connect with each other through the vulnerability of our own stories.

Looking back, I'm so grateful for this long and winding journey. There is so much value in the unique combination of my beautiful sexuality and my fragile faith. They blend together to make a specific pair of glasses through which I see the world. It allows me to see colors and beauty I don't think I would see otherwise.

Exodus International and most gay conversion therapy practices in the US and Canada have since shut down. However, there are still ministries out there that claim you can "pray the gay away." I would encourage anyone to seek counseling to work through issues, but I don't believe it's healthy to try to change our sexuality. Whatever your faith, you can find places that are accepting and affirming of your whole identity. Today, Tams and I belong to an affirming Christian church in Maple Ridge, British Columbia, called Open Door Church.

A few words about my relationship with my parents today. Since getting married and having our two kids, it's been an up-and-down journey. I have always fought for a relationship with them, but we have been very careful about having boundaries. It is also much easier to maintain a relationship living in different provinces. We will probably never agree on the gay Christian issue. But we have all come a long way, we love each other, and they are Nana and Papa to our kids. So we keep trying to do life together the best we can. I believe there are some relationships that are worth holding the tension and learning what it means to love each other while strongly holding different beliefs. I have learned that life can be both heartbreaking and beautiful in the same moment. My only job is to live authentically and love as best I can. Life is short, and love is powerful.

During my years of struggle, I was much too afraid to seek out any resources that I would have deemed as "non-Christian." There were no "gay Christian" resources like there are today. If you are struggling with reconciling your faith and sexuality, there are now organizations and books that can help. Please reach out, don't give up, and find a community of support. You are not alone. We are all in this together.

Thank you for sharing in my journey.

I look forward to hearing about yours!

—Stace

Resources

Websites:

- BelovedArise.org

- FaithfullyLGBT.com

- GayChristian.net

- InsideOutFaith.org

- OutChristian.com

- Q Christian Fellowship   https://www.qchristian.org

- QueerGrace.com

- The Reformation Project - https://www.reformationproject.org/

Books:

- *Bad Theology Kills: Undoing Toxic Belief & Reclaiming Your Spiritual Authority* by Kevin Garcia

- *Does Jesus Really Love Me?: A Gay Christian's Pilgrimage in Search of God in America* by Jeff Chu

- *God and the Gay Christian: The Biblical Case in Support of Same-Sex Relationships* by Matthew Vines

- *Queerfully and Wonderfully Made: A Guide for LGBTQ+ Christian Teens* edited by Leigh Finke

- *Torn: Rescuing the Gospel from the Gays-vs.-Christians Debate* by Justin Lee

- *Transforming: The Bible and the Lives of Transgender Christians* by Austen Hartke

- *Unashamed: A Coming Out Guide for LGBTQ Christians* by Amber Cantorna

- *Undivided: Coming Out, Becoming Whole, and Living Free from Shame* by Vicky Beeching

- *Walking the Bridgeless Canyon: Repairing the Breach between the Church and the LGBT Community* by Kathy Baldock

Acknowledgments

I am indebted to so many people who helped me along the journey of creating this book.

To Rachel Held Evans, you were one of the first people I shared my idea with. Your gentle, loving encouragement was the boost of courage I needed to truly begin this journey. Thank you for loving all of us LGBTQ Christians well, Rachel. You are deeply missed.

To Jennifer Knapp—I tried not to fangirl you on our phone conversation! When I shared this idea with you, you had such confidence that this was not strange, but in fact great. Thank you—our conversation was a real turning point for me.

To Hillary McBride, for your ongoing support and encouragement along this journey, and beyond.

To my Pizza Palz on "Design Island"—Kora Kosicka & Kiersten Eagan. Thank you both for being there at the very beginning, and sharing in my excitement. You both held steadfast to the belief that "this was going somewhere." Kora—thank you for our many walks and talks over green curry in 2020. Your continued insight and friendship has meant the world to me.

To the core team at Doberman Pictures—Dallas, Craig, Meg, Jim, Garnet, and Rod. Thank you for believing in me, and for your support as I worked on this outside of our ongoing productions! It's an honor to be a part of your studio.

To my agent, Claire Draper, and the team at The Bent Agency. Claire, I truly value your insight and support, ever since our first phone conversation. Thank you for believing in me. I know without your help and guidance, this book would not be possible.

To Naomi Krueger, thank you for taking care of my story so well. It has been a true pleasure working alongside you.

To Kim Ito—thank you for your friendship, laughs and support along this winding road. "Less walking more talking" forever!

To Justin Lee—thank you for your courage. You were one of the first gay Christians I ever heard about. Your ministry has been integral to me. Your authentic heart and gentle openness has been such an incredible example. I am lucky to call you a friend.

To my friends who read versions of this along the way, gave feedback, cried with me, laughed with me, and just kept loving me: Tracy Dumka, Tammy Wood, Jen Armstrong, Missi McKown, Crystal and Wendi Newman, and Megan Huizing. Thank you, I love you all so much.

To my kids, my hearts, Robson and Hudson. You are both still pretty young to understand what I keep needing to go into my office to work on. But your enthusiastic hugs and "Great job, Mommy!" have sometimes been the only reason I can get anything done. I love you both more than I can properly express.

To my wife Tams. What a wild adventure our life together has been so far, hey? Thank you for always supporting me, and for believing hard enough for us both. What a rare privilege it is, to be loved so well by you.

Stacey Chomiak is an artist in the animation industry, getting her start on the well-loved series My Little Pony: Friendship is Magic. While she continues to lend her talents to various children's animated shows, she also illustrates children's books. She lives with her family happily nestled amid the tall trees of the West Coast of Canada. Stacey identifies as a gay Christian and loves to advocate for the LGBTQ community and have conversations around faith and sexuality. When she isn't furiously sketching, Stacey is likely to be out for a jog, critiquing her favorite Hitchcock film, or encouraging her children to dance with her to Whitney Houston.